Property of
Charles A. Owen Jr.
Medieval Studies Library

SCOTTISH WRITERS

Editor
DAVID DAICHES

ROBERT HENRYSON

by Matthew P. McDiarmid

This study of one of Scotland's great "makars" sets Henryson clearly in the world of fifteenth century Scotland and Europe, illuminating both his Scottishness and his relation to literary, religious and philosophical themes and traditions that were available to him. Mr. McDiarmid uses all traceable clues to Henryson's identity and career, but most of all he is concerned with his poetic art and the cultural world that nurtured it. Henryson's uniqueness is stressed at least as much as the heritage he shared with other writers: the differences, for example, between his mode of writing and feeling and that of Chaucer are developed at a number of points. This is an essential guide-book for anyone wishing to come to terms with a great Scottish poet.

ROBERT HENRYSON

MATTHEW P. McDIARMID

SCOTTISH ACADEMIC PRESS

EDINBURGH

Published by
Scottish Academic Press Ltd.
33 Montgomery Street, Edinburgh EH7 5JX

First published 1981
SBN 7073 0306 0

Printed in Great Britain by
Clark Constable Ltd.,
Hopetoun Street, Edinburgh

CONTENTS

ACKNOWLEDGMENT

The Scottish Academic Press acknowledges the financial assistance of the Scottish Arts Council in the publication of this volume.

CHAPTER I

ROBERT HENRYSON c. 1436–c. 1503:
FACTS AND SPECULATIONS

It is perhaps always a mistake to think that the poetical personality admired or liked on the printed page must have made the same impression in the circumstances of real life, or that further knowledge of the poet's career must recommend him yet more. Known cases vary in their effect; the actual members of the 'gens irritabile vatum' may disappoint, and the mythic pictures of our poetical heroes that ignorance allows us to paint may flatter, yet it is at least a tribute to the part of them that means most that one does want to know more. Certainly the present writer would like to know more about Robert Henryson as he lived outside his verse than about any other Scots poet. The knowledge of that kind that we do possess derives from a few references, some related facts, and some relevant and reasonable guesses.

Departing from the usual order of such narratives, we begin the biographic argument, for that is what it must be, with the small nucleus of fact that his later and middle years provide, and from there work backwards in time.

In the poem best known, if misleadingly, as *The Lament for the Makaris* Dunbar tells us that death has talked with the poet in Dunfermline,

> In Dunfermelyne he hes done roune
> With Maister Robert Henrisoune.

The notice is preceded by the name of "Roull of Corstorphine', who wrote his amusing rant *Roule Cursing* some time between 1492 and 1503, and before that by 'Merseir

Quha did in luf so lifly write' who is probably the William Merser who figures in the royal *Accounts* 1500. The names that follow that of Henryson, those of Sir John Ross of Montgrenan in Ayrshire, who died in late 1493, and 'last of aw' John Reid of Stobo and Quentin Shaw of Dreghorn in Ayrshire who both died in 1505, come together probably only because they were particular friends and associates of Dunbar at court. It would seem that Henryson's death should be placed only a year or two before 1505. That he was a master of arts, as the title invariably indicates, will be noted.

One employment is stated in Robert Lekpreuik's print of *The Morall Fabillis* at Edinburgh 1569, 'Maister Robert Henrison, Scholemaister at Dunfermeling'. Doubtless that position is specified because it carried authority, Aesop's beast fables being often used as an entertaining accompaniment to instruction in the Latin language, and so respectable a post assured the godly customer of the now Reformed capital that he was purchasing more than the idle tales popular with youth, 'raveries' as Alexander Hume, author of the pious and beautiful *Day Estivall* was to call them. The motives of the publisher Henry Charteris in obtruding a fact only marginally relevant to the work—for we cannot imagine Henryson primarily aiming his poetical inventions at the boys he taught, any more than at the 'Lord Of quhome the Name it neidis not record'—are mentioned here because of the extraordinary effect of his description. It has excessively and foolishly haunted biography and criticism, and has actually been brought in to support the mistaken notion of a locally limited experience—as the one-time schoolmaster (so the best evidence suggests) Shakespeare dubiously observes, 'home-keeping youths have ever homely wits'—and narrowly didactic personality. The contrast, implicit or explicit, in such a misconception is usually with that travelled, courtly and knowledgeable man of the world, Geoffrey Chaucer.

Robert Henryson was, however, a more travelled man than Chaucer and, as might be said of so many educated Scots in these days, had resided abroad much longer. His later experience and employments were varied enough.

In the first place he was also a practising lawyer. He had been appointed to his schoolmastership by Richard Bothwell, head of Dunfermline's Benedictine abbey, like the poet himself a bachelor in canon law; and beyond question it is the poet as notary public (*Magistro Roberto Henrison publico notario*) who witnesses three of the charters of the new abbot, Henry Crichton (1472–82), conveying the feu of Spittalfield beside Inverkeithing to an Edinburgh burgess Patrick Baron, whose name will recur in this account. The charters are dated 18, 19 March and 6 July 1478, and are also witnessed by Fife notables like Sir John Lundy and John, baron of Balfour.[1] Regrettably his lawyer's protocol book, that is, case-book, unlike that of Gavin Ros the schoolmaster at Ayr, has not survived. Had it done so, it would have recorded his involvement in the many transactions, mainly property and money deals but not wholly—there were also the testaments, pious donations, anything requiring a binding oath—of all kinds and ranks of persons. He may have attended the King's Council with the Lord Abbot, even assisted him in governmental negotiations, and would have represented clients in the courts that he so familiarly satirizes in his fables. It will be remembered that at the centre of Cresseid's tragedy in the *Testament* is a court scene that Mercurius as 'foirspeikar' attends 'With buik in hand' and 'pen and ink to report all reddie', and that the assembly of 'the fourfut-tit beistis' has 'the pointis of ane parliament'. His school, his pupils may have thought appropriately, stood near the burgh Tolbooth (Townhouse and court-room) just north of 'the commone gait' or main street, and Henryson would have functioned in both buildings; as did his successor in the Grammar School John Moffat—during the former's lifetime, as John Durkan suggests, probably his under-

teacher, whose help would let him pursue his other
concerns—the author of the very popular comic poem *The
Wife of Auchtermuchty*.[2]

But with his office of schoolmaster would go other
duties. He would be expected occasionally to serve the
abbot at 'tymes of hie solempne festival . . . at hie mes and
evinsang', as the Master at Edinburgh served the abbot of
Holyrood;[3] like Moffat to be chaplain of one of the many
altars, and when available to take 'the morne service'. He
would also visit regularly St Leonard's hospital for lepers
on the south side of the town. The other patron saint of
lepers was St Ninian, and so we find the Master of the
Grammar School at Glasgow being responsible for both
the physical and spiritual comfort of the patients in the
hospital there.[4] From this distressing duty would come the
experience of the disease that is so terribly and feelingly
described in the *Testament*.

The annual pay of a schoolmaster, taking into account
his supporting chaplaincy, and accepting the analogy of
Aberdeen and Ayr, was a little over ten pounds,[5] not a
great sum even in those days. He was not a whole-time
lawyer so such fees as came his way would be welcome.
Also, as in the monastery, of course, so later in the abbot's
new schoolhouse, board may have been provided. He
seems to have considered himself fortunate in his circumstances, like his country mouse 'content with small
possessioun'.

One poem, 'On fut by Forth as I couth found' (took my
walk), and the delightfully fresh descriptions of springtide
and harvest-time—he is one, he tells us in 'The Preiching
of the Swallow', 'that luifit corn' and marked the time
when 'Columbie up keikis throw the clay'—in an exceptionally beautiful countryside, remind us of a different
satisfaction that he knew.

There is indeed a contrast with the life-styles of both
Chaucer and Dunbar, servants of their respective courts,
the Englishman much the more well endowed in this

world's goods, and it is a contrast not altogether to their advantage. Of course, Henryson was as acquainted with men and places as either of these poets; more important, his particular range of practical, religious and social services was for the most part outwith their experience, a difference that is reflected in their several concerns and sensibilities. The two poets who were king's servants, one highly connected in English society, the other of a noble family that, as Kennedy knew, was descended from the pre-Conquest earls of Northumbria, however 'on evil days fallen', do not care to dwell on the wrongs of the unprivileged, to find time to observe that a labouring life could be 'half ane purgatory', or reflect on the yet more dreadful aspects of experience that Cresseid knew.

When we leave Dunfermline, in the backwards course of this sketchy narrative, the account of the poet's life at certain points becomes less certain, and what the reader must sometimes be asked to consider is only the most probable of guesses.

In the *Munimenta*, II. 69, of what was then the new University of Glasgow, founded in 1451 at the instance of bishop William Turnbull, there appears this entry, *Anno Domini lxii die decimo mensis Septembris incorporatus fuit venerabilis vir Magister Robertus Henrisone in artibus licenciatus et in decretis bachalarius*: 'On the 10th September 1462 an honourable man Master Robert Henryson, being master in arts and bachelor in canon law, was admitted a member of the university'. Unless this be the exception, and there is no reason to think that it is, like all other mentions of a Master Robert Henryson in the records of the second half of the fifteenth century, the reference is to the poet. It is at least as acceptable as the identification of Walter Kennedy at Glasgow, William Dunbar and Gavin Douglas at St Andrews. That Henryson does not otherwise appear in the well kept records of either university shows that he did not attend them as a student. The notice agrees, of course, with his later practice as a lawyer and with his concerned accounts of malpractice in the Scottish courts. As for the term *venerabilis*, its application is purely formal, without reference to age, cases of Scotsmen receiving the description in their late twenties and early thirties, in Scottish and other universities, being not uncommon.

Evidently the legal qualification, obtained abroad as was the 'masterate', was the motivating factor in his arrival at, and admission to, the university. James Coutts, and perhaps tacitly its more recent historian John Durkan, assume that the poet had come to study, pre-sumably to advance to the further degree of doctor of decreets (the Scots term for canon law),[6] but the first decade or so of studying law at Glasgow shows no clear case of arrivals from abroad simply for such a purpose, though more than one member of the scanty teaching establishment does use his position to seek and duly acquire that distinction. Canon law was at no time so vigorous and attractive a Faculty at Glasgow as the assumption suggests. The University, particularly its Rector, David Cadyow, who was there licensed in decreets in 1460, was anxious to remedy the situation. To that end Cadyow made a bequest 2 March 1463 of twelve Scottish merks for the provision of 'an excellent, worthy and fit', clerk to give 'matins' lectures, *de mane legenti*, the 'reader' to say mass daily for the soul of the donor at the Virgin's altar in the lower church of the cathedral.[7] The Latin phrase is interesting. Durkan supposes that Cadyow hoped to attract a doctor, but at Paris at least there was a distinction between bachelors, described as *Legentes de mane*, who lectured on the Decretals at 'matins', and doctors who read at 'prime'.[7] Someone with Henryson's degree was intended, and I suggest that his coming was anticipated, and it was the poet who filled Cadyow's lectureship; also that it was the hope of such an appointment more than the continuance of studies, though that would be expected, that attracted Henryson.

If he did benefit by the bequest and perform the conditional service, he must have been ordained as a priest. A reserved benefice was then the equivalent of a modern 'student's grant' to make study possible, especially abroad, and did not commit the beneficiary to major orders—there is no evidence that Henryson enjoyed one—but the terms of the bequest did. Later in his career to be at once priest, notary and schoolmaster, would have been no uncommon union of functions. As Dr Leslie Macfarlane has observed to me, necessity and the competition of their too numerous kind forced clerics to seek subsistence from many quarters. That the poet was a churchman, as were Dunbar and Douglas, need hardly surprise us, and is what his subsequent duties would lead us to expect. It agrees, of course, with the prevailing concern of his poetry.

Since there is no further mention of him in the Glasgow records, which are defective for canon law, we cannot say when he left the city. There is, however, the likelihood that had he stayed long, in his case, for example, the five years or so that would have brought him to the doctorate, his presence would have been noted in one or other of the university's *congregationes*, which were effectively meetings of the dominant Faculty of Arts. That body took heed of actions and promotions in the much less thriving Faculty. Obviously he did not take the more advanced degree, and left Glasgow some time before 1468. In that year the abbot of Dunfermline petitioned for a house to accommodate his schoolmaster.[8] We do not know that the position refers to Henryson, who may well have gone abroad again for a few years of further study. If it does refer to him, we must suppose that about 1465 he took up his post at Dunfermline, being lodged in the monastery until the new accommodation became available.

Several considerations may have prompted the move. As we shall see, Fife may have been his native county. The security of a lifetime appointment, as all such appointments then were, may have appealed to him. If access to books counted with him, while Glasgow's cathedral had an excellent library (notably it possessed a copy of the commentary of Nicholas Trivet on Boethius's *De Consolatione* that he was to use in his *Orpheus*), certainly the abbey was also well supplied in that respect. Bothwell's interest in Scottish history is remembered nowadays for the *Liber Pluscardensis* that he commissioned in 1461 from a monk who had attended on both Joan of Arc and the Scottish Dauphiness.[9] There were the libraries of local families like the Erskines and the Balfours, and in any case St Andrews and Edinburgh were not many miles distant. He would certainly be nearer the centre of Scottish events, political and cultural. Also, the church, monastery and king's palace, at Dunfermline had a special prestige. In the church were buried Malcolm Canmore and his queen Saint Margaret, the greatest of their sons David I, Robert Bruce with his son David II, and Bruce's great lieutenant Randolph earl of Moray; James I king and poet had been born in the palace, and both the contemporary monarchs, James III and James IV were visitors.

As a man to be employed in business affairs by the abbot, and other landlords, he would have made sure of receiving at this time, either from Glasgow's bishop or from Bothwell, authority to act as an Apostolic notary public. Imperial or, as they were after the Act of 1469, royal notaries could not practice in ecclesiastical as well as civil courts. Henryson shows familiarity with both, and it is a 'consistorie' that is described in the caustic 'Taill of the Scheip and the Doig.'

From which continental university or universities did the poet fetch his degrees? Not the English ones, though a Scot might visit them, as did the theologian and historian John Mair on his way to France. MacQueen suggests the University of Rome (where indeed Gilbert Rerik the arch-deacon of Glasgow had studied law) on the simple ground that in 'The Taill of the Lyoun and the Mous', without textual authority a visionary Aesop who is now 'in hevin for ay' and therefore without his traditionary deformities, claims to have read 'civile law' at Rome. The suggestion is interesting; a visit to Italy is not improbable and would explain why he remembers the wines of Italy along with those of France in his *Preiching*. But Henryson's degree was in canon law, and the fiction is sufficiently explained by his use of the 'Romulus' version and his desire to give a shadow of Roman and ecclesiastical authority to the fabulist, when he discourses on a breach of civil justice by slothful king and rebellious subject in Scotland. The most common recourse of students of canon law was Paris. Unfortunately the records of that Faculty have been lost, and his absence from those of the Faculty of Arts, mostly preserved, indicates that his M.A. at least was not obtained there. The other French university most attended by Scots, though specially for its famous school of civil law, Orleans, is defective in its extant lists of names, and the almost equally popular universities of Louvain and Köln, which have fuller matriculation rolls, both showing the attendance of founding members of Glasgow University, have no evident claim on a Robert Henryson. He may have gone elsewhere, though search for his name has been unsuccessful.[10] Certainly he resided in France for a considerable time, as is shown by the several French sources of his poetry, and the present writer *chooses* to imagine him at Paris for a period. Possible kinsmen, to be mentioned again, who had a connection with the Sorbonne, are a Master Robert Henryson, not otherwise noticed, who in 1429 acted for the university and its Nation of Germans and Scots in a difficult lawsuit,[11] and a Master James Henryson who graduated there in 1484.

The degrees that recommended the poet to Glasgow in September 1462 are the only evidence that should be considered in suggesting the period of his birth. The procedure of Paris was fairly representative of that of other

European universities, and does not disagree with normal practice at Glasgow and St Andrews; a residence of almost five years was expected for the 'masterate', the stipulation of a further period of teaching being frequently dispensed, especially with noble or foreign students; and there was a further stay of about the same duration for the baccalaureate in canon law.[12] As Paris was papally forbidden to teach civil law, a supplementary visit to Orleans (such as the future Bishop Elphinstone made) or to Angers was not uncommon. Consequently, since matriculation usually occurred about the age of fifteen, the poet's birth-year should have been close to 1436. The guesses of his editor Harvey Wood and of John MacQueen, which respectively propose dates in the third and second decades of the century are merely impressionistic.[13]

About his native region we can only guess reasonably, noticing the more relevant-seeming considerations. That he should make for Glasgow rather than St Andrews on his return may be due only to the opportunity above-mentioned, his awareness of the virtual failure of, or apparent want of esteem for, legal studies within the older university, and the evident determination (also eventually fruitless) of the Glasgow founders to establish an effective school of law. It was the statutes of Bologna that originally they examined most seriously, though Turnbull's successor Andrew of Durisdeer had taken his licentiate at Paris and been intimate there with the reforming cardinal d'Estouteville. There is nothing, however, to suggest even remotely a west-country connection. On the other hand there are strong indications that he was simply going home when round about 1465 he settled in Dunfermline. What I have been able to learn about schoolmasters at this period points to local men being preferred for the office. Increasingly the burgh, probably therefore the neighbouring magnates, sought to have a say in the appointment, as is illustrated by the defensive litigation of Master John

Henryson in 1573, despite his having been notary and keeper of the abbey charters—the latter possibly another responsibility of the poet—from before 1555.[14]

In that district of Fife, especially beside the near-by port of Inverkeithing, there was an exceptional concentration of persons with the poet's surname. David Laing's observation that it is to be found in many parts of Scotland is quite true, but also as regards proportionate mention in the records quite misleading. One group of related persons at least deserves mention. Between 1450 and 1511 its leading members were all concerned to establish themselves as land-owners in the above-mentioned area. John Henryson a law-officer, Serjeant of Fordell two miles NNE Inverkeithing, as also of Edinburgh's Canongate and Prestonpans, was for long a baillie and 'custumar' of the port, and from at least 1465 had land at Fordell. He died in the late 1490s, about the same time as Robert Henryson, probably his brother, a very busy merchant of Edinburgh who purchased Mill Dam and other lands near Fordell. James Henryson, Robert's son, the already mentioned graduate of Paris, was successively King's Advocate, Justice Clerk, and in 1511 baron of Fordell.[15] For a time he had been the abbot's baillie. That the poet belonged to this family cannot be asserted but it is quite likely that he was related to it. Certainly as notary, and servant of their 'superior', the abbot of Dunfermline, he knew these land-hungry persons well. The Spittalfield whose purchase he witnesses in 1478 adjoins Fordell.

With such speculations this lamentably insubstantial review of evidence from outside the poetry ends but a last wholly unsupported one may be indulged. Was the poet who understood Venus so well, who could write, though in a religious context (*Annunciation*, 1), the line, 'Forcy as deith is likand lufe', one of the many legitimated sons of the priesthood? Is it worthwhile wondering whether he was the son of that earlier Master Robert Henryson at Paris, as bishop William Elphinstone was the son of

Master William Elphinstone, cleric, lecturer at Glasgow,
one-time student and love-poet at Louvain;[16] and as
Master William Dunbar, almost certainly a cadet of the
Dunbars of Biel (hence his friend Kennedy's jest that he
was one of Belzebub's children) is likely to have been the
son of the Master William Dunbar of that family recorded
in 1440? Giving the son the father's Christian name was
much more the usual practice than it is today.

   In this retrospective way the line—it is scarcely more—
of the poet's life has been traced from his death a little after
1500 to his birth about 1436, an extent of some sixty five
years. The points that most significantly mark that
temporal line are, of course, his poems, and their agree-
ment with the above narrative has to be considered.
Unfortunately their placing involves uncertainties and
'reasonable suggestions' no less than do some of the
physical events that have been reviewed. He was not so
often the topical and occasional poet that the courtly
circumstances of Dunbar demanded. He was self-
revelatory in a much more general way, both as regards
himself and his society; and his works did not have the
ambitious length that made Gavin Douglas, after the
manner of his day, scrupulous to date them precisely.
Something, however, can be said.

   The latest poem for which a date naturally presents
itself is *Ane Prayer for the Pest*, a cry from the heart that was
almost certainly compelled by the most dreadful plague of
the century, one that in 1498–99 closed both schools and
churches, making the burghers of Dunfermline take the
ineffective action of forbidding victuals to be sold outside
the town 'induryne the tyme of this plage';[17] so mortally
infectious that, as Henryson declared, 'nane dar mak with
uthir residence' and men could 'dye as beistis without
confessioun'. It is brought into the dating colophon of the
anonymous translation, 'the buik of King Alexander the
Conquerour', completed August 1499: 'Into this realme
there rang a pestilence fell./Thair was na man that had

into memor/That ever hard tell of sic ane plaige
before'.[18] And it is mentioned by Alexander Mylne in
his Latin 'Lives of the Bishops of Dunkeld'. Sometimes it
is called 'the Het siknes'. If Henryson survived it, it was
not for long.

Concerning the *Testament* a first observation is that it
was blatantly used by a M[aster] G. Myll', writing at St
Andrews in his little prose treatise *The Spectackle of Luf*, a
peculiarly unconvincing and well illustrated discourse on
the evils of lechery that dates itself 10 July 1492.[19] Master
Myll pretends to have a Latin original before him, but the
reader should view the claim as he does Henryson's
reference of his invention to

> ane uther quair
> In quhilk I fand the fatall destenie
> Of fair Cresseid that endit wretchitlie.

And he will remember these lines and stanza 11 of the
poem particularly when he reads how Cresseid 'went
commoun amang the grekis And syne deid in gret mysere
& pane'. The prose-writer's self-description, 'ald hars and
dotand' and no longer able to 'mak the service' of love,
should also recall the poet's sad avowal that he is 'ane man
of age' in whom love 'kindillis nocht sa sone as in
youthheid', followed at once by the wry jest that he has
had to learn the value of drink as an aphrodisiac, 'To help
be Phisike quhair that nature faillit'. That either writer
was wholly serious about his age and necessary preference
of a good book to love-making may be doubted. None the
less, in a time that classified the so-called ages of man
pedantically the phrase 'ane man of age' referred to the
years between fifty and sixty,[20] and the spirit and manner
of the *Testament* do suggest a man in his maturity. Since I
find no reason in the text for Denton Fox's distinction
between poet and narrator, a simple calculation should
place the poem about 1486–1490.

Near the same time should come *Sum Practisis of*

Medecyne. The meaning of lines 1–6 has been oddly over-looked. The poem is a 'flyting' with a poetical doctor friend who would 'ruffill me with a ryme', and is apparently treating Henryson for dysentery, and it or the friend's jesting is obviously the source of the ludicrous tradition of the manner of the poet's dying that was reported to Sir Francis Kinaston in 1639.[21] Thomas Erskine, earl of Kelly (whose ancestor requested the version of *Alexander* done by Sir Gilbert Hay in 1438, a fact stated in the 1499 translation) the reporter, had his principal lands in Fife and may there have picked up the story, according to which Henryson died of 'the flux' shortly after the effort of spending some four-letter words on a wise old woman who had come with an infallible remedy: he was to go three times 'widdershins' (the opposite of the sun's motion) round the rowan-tree in his garden. The poem was clever and amusing enough to set a fashion in flyting poetry. It shows, however, no awareness of the fantastic possibilities for mutual abuse that Kennedy and Dunbar develop in 1491–92. The reluctant Dunbar particularly indicates that he and his challenging friend are not the first to enter this not too 'sanitary' field.

Another minor poem *The Bludy Serk* seems capable of a more precise dating. It is an allegory of religious loyalty couched in the terms of heroic romance but the titular phrase, several times repeated in the text, for example the last line, 'Think on the bludy serk', renders the *arma sanguinolenta* of the main source, the *Gesta Romanorum,* and may well have a topical reference. In September 1489 Lord Forbes marched south under the banner of what was called 'the bludy sark' [shirt] of the dead James III.[22]

Henryson's *Morall Fabillis*, the most extensive of his works, might well be expected to comment on the contemporary scene, social and political, and a few such comments do occur. Similarly one or two sources should provide information. In this respect, however, the *Fabillis* presents a problem; it is not the simple unitary composition that some critics have considered it, to be adequately dated by the latest reference.

The few clearly political allusions are to strife between king and subjects in the late 70s but particularly the ensuing and final decade of James's reign. One has been convincingly identified by the historian Ranald Nicholson. In 'The Taill of the Lyoun and the Mous' the poet appeals to the reader's knowledge of recent events, and ends his discourse with a prayer that 'tressoun of this cuntrie be exyld'. He knows that 'king and lord may weill wit quhat I mene'. In the tale the lion-king—the royal standard was the lion rampant—sleeps as if dead, and so lets the humblest of his subjects play about him. On waking, his merciful remission of the offence of the little captive, whom he sets free—James's weakening of the authority of law by such 'remissions', in this case lucky, was a common cause of complaint from parliament and poets alike—wins a response from its kind, and they later loose the lion from the 'presoun' prepared for him by vengeful 'rurall men' who could not forget the injuries and depredation done by him, 'For hurt men wrytis in the marbill stane'.

James III was much better known in his capital than out of it; his seizure to the crown of inheritances small and great, failure to give consistent justice, and attempt to strengthen his position with a policy of English marriages, made powerful enemies. The nobles, summoned to an army meant to recover Berwick from English hands, and avenge the insult done by the English king in breaking off marriage negotiations and requiring repayment of Princess Margaret's dowry, at Lauder Brig seized James and warded him in Edinburgh castle. His banished brother, the Duke of Albany, who had been forced to nourish his own secret ambitions, returned and led the citizens to the siege of the castle and the liberation of the king. As a reward for this, and financial help in meeting English demands, on 16th November 1482 the men of

Edinburgh were granted two charters of privilege, Provost Walter Bertram receiving a life-time pension. Bertram, like his already-mentioned fellow burgess Patrick Baron, who preceded him as Provost, would be known to Henryson as a purchaser of feus from the abbot of Dunfermline.[23]

Another, equally plain, allusion to Lauder Brig and events thereafter is intended in 'The Taill of the Wolf and the Wedder'. The shepherd's sturdy old hound had kept the 'selie beistis' safe from the wolf. When the hound dies, a ram boldly tries to 'counterfait the doig' by wearing its skin, but in a chase loses its disguise and is killed. It is interesting that in his political fable *Rob Stenes Dreme* (1591) Alexander Montgomerie was later to use another fable of the dog, sheep and wolves, to rebuke James VI for out-lawing his cousin and alleged defender Frances earl of Bothwell, and preferring the counsel of Secretary Maitland.[24] Henryson seems to be questioning the wisdom of exiling Albany and the now ageing earl of Douglas, who were both threatening the Borders in March–July 1482. The fatally pretentious ram would be the king's low-born and aggressively prospering servant Thomas Cochrane, who was hanged, along with another favourite Thomas Preston, in July 1482. The reference is made quite clear in the poet's *moralitas*: there are 'pure men' who will 'counterfute ane lord in all degre', who will 'lichtlie [scorn] lordis in their deidis' and who forget that 'It settis [befits] na servand for to uphald weir' [war]; their punishment will come and 'sum man tit [trip] thair heillis over thair heid'.[25] The political alignment here is very close to that of Hary in his *Wallace* (1476–78), though it would have been the leadership and not the war with Scotland's 'auld enemies' that he found fault with.[26]

Both fables strongly suggest a reaction to recent happenings, yet it would be a hasty assumption that placed them, much less all the fables, at precisely this period. Comment on such revolutionary doings would be just as natural a year or two later. And what are we to think of certain stanzas at the beginning of the 'Parliament', and indeed of the whole of its remarkable sequence of incidents? It is difficult not to have in mind the situation of the young James IV as rebel and therefore 'airt and pairt' in the killing of his father, crowned the same year 1488, which is also the year of his first parliament, 6th October, held to debate the causes of the late king's death and exonerate the causers, when one reads the fox's words over his father's body—

> Thankand grit God off that conclusioun,
> And said, "Now sall I bruke, sen I am air,
> The boundis quhair thow wes wont for to
>   repair".

What did the young prince think of the father who so neglected a saintly mother,[27] and what did loyalists think of the young prince in that violent year? Accepting my timing of Henryson's 'Parliament', one has to wonder whether the 'contumax' mare who refuses to attend it corresponds to the northern and western recalcitrants (the lords Forbes, Huntly, Darnley, Lisle) of 1488–89.

So far as topical allusions help, it seems that certain fables should have been written at least as early as 1482, others at least as late as 1489, and probably we should view the collection as being intermittently composed and over a slightly more extensive period, 1480–1490.

The literary sources support this tentative dating. Laments in the fables seem to echo those in *Wallace* in parodic fashion: the lion's lament in its captivity, "Quha sall me bute? Quha sall my bandis brek?/Quha sall me put fra pane of this presoun?" (1536–41), seems to recollect Wallace's lament in the same plight and Hary's lament for Scotland left leaderless (II, 198–200, XII. 1119–23). And the same laments may be farcically echoed by the hen Pertok when Chanticlere is supposed slain, "Quha sall our lemman be? Quha sall us leid? . . . Now

efter him, allace, how sall we leif?'' (502–8). For a more
serious and impressive effect Hary's portrait of Wallace,
and award of a place in heaven to the great patriot, suggest
Henryson's unprecedented description of Aesop in 'The
Taill of the Lyon and the Mous'. Here the memory of
Wallace was very relevant to the political topic.
Alternatively one might wonder if Hary remembers the
fox at confession, "For to repent my mind can not con-
cluid,/Bot of this thing, that I haiff slane sa few", when he
makes Wallace actually smile at his English confessor's
question, "than thou rapentis nocht?", and reply, "I
grant part Inglismen I slew,/In my quarell me thocht
nocht half enew" (XII. 1379–86). But it is simpler and
safer to assume that in all these cases it is Henryson who
remembers the unforgettable work composed in 1476–78
by the neighbouring poet.[28]

That he had read Caxton's *History of Reynarde the Foxe*,
which came out in 1481, is possible but dubious since the
one argument for it that has any particular force is the fact
that 'Waytskaith', the name of the wolf that hears the fox's
confession, is said in the *History*, obscurely and *en passant* as
if the English writer had a source in mind, to belong to a
clerical cousin at Rome. Caxton is unlikely to have
invented it, and both writers may have found it, or a name
that suggested it, in some more specific context no longer
known to us. It is economical, however, if verbally not
evident to suppose that Henryson read both the tales,
'The Wolf and the Wedder' and 'the wolf in the schadow
of the Mone', in Caxton's *Aesop* 1484, though he might
have found them in other and separate sources, particularly French, and hit naturally on similar
phraseology. If he did fetch the first of these fables from
Caxton, this would not contradict my suggestion of a
reference in the *Moralitas* to the violent events of 1482,
though it is my impression that the allusion is topical.

A final item in this review of dating evidence in the
Fabillis is its use by the unknown author of *The Tale of*

Cokelbie Sow, a fantastic piece of comic moralising in what the writer calls 'mad mouthing metre'. It was a popular novelty when Douglas cited it in his *Palyce of Honour* written 1500–1501, and Dunbar speaks of it a little later in his *Remonstrance*. It has 'Waitscath' from one fable and the hens' names 'Toppok' (better the Reynardian 'Coppok') and 'Sprutok' from 'Chanticleir and the Foxe'. That Henryson is the debtor here as MacQueen supposes,[29] is not the simplest or most probable view. The connection merely supports the opinion that the *Fabillis* was completed about 1490.

The reader may well find this argumentation tedious enough, but it has the interest of representing these remarkable beast creations as not comprising a work proposed and executed 'at one go', but as a collection of separate tales, separately meditated, composed and even revised over a considerable span of years, perhaps from the late seventies, more probably from about 1480, to near 1490 when the author abandoned rather than completed the series, in the process, or finally, giving a semblance of unitary purpose—the sufficient unity was the beast-world as Henryson so humanly imagined and moralized it—by developing his 'Prolog' in the way of the French *Ysopets*, supplying a linkage only where a special point such as the above-noted fox's response to his father's death was to be made.

The slight revisionary aspect of the *Fabillis* deserves this notice, not only because it touches on the question of date but also because, as the present writer should know, editors tend to think too simply of the careful and not so careful scribe, of 'the better reading'. Thus in his really valuable review of Henryson's text Professor MacQueen provides evidence of such revision while talking only in these terms.

About the period of the *Orpheus and Erudices* successive suggestions have been offered by MacQueen: firstly that it was written at Glasgow because the cathedral library held a copy of the poem's main source, Nicholas Trivet's widely known gloss on the *De Consolatione* of Boethius; secondly that it was written at Dunfermline some time after 1469, the date of Marsilio Ficino's commentary on Plato's *Symposium*, knowledge of which is unconvincingly, if interestingly, said to be found in the poem.[31] More notable are the two lines 342–43 that put in hell 'Abbotis and men of all religioun/For evill disponyng of thar placis rent'. Henry Crichton was intruded as abbot 1472–1482 by royal influence, and in the year of his appointment sold a nineteen-year lease of the rents of Stirling parish for more than five hundred pounds.[32] Henryson was a man of independent mind and was probably always quite capable of sending his abbot to hell on sound religious grounds, but Crichton, as observed, is almost certainly the 'lord' who later encouraged the composition of the fables. There is at least reason for considering a date between 1465 and 1472, when as one of the 'tendouris of the young and insolent' (his own phrase in the *Orpheus*) he was not long settled in Dunfermline. This agrees with the lyric and emotive felicity that certain lines have in their context, the hint that they convey of the author's own enjoyment of such sensuous verse, features that are naturally if unnecessarily associated with fairly youthful writing—

"Quhar art thou gane, my luf Erudices?"	(143)
Into the mone he maid no residens	(216)
Passing all instrumentis musicall	(221)
"Thy lippis red, to kiss delicious"	(356)

If I have tediously laboured the question of the dating of the sadly slight remains of Henryson's variously impressive work, it is not only for confirmation of the limits of his career as given by other evidence. Such poetical dates as are available raise a question about the apparent failure of verse in the period when poets are usually supposed to discover their gift, in their youth. Doubtless the simple answer is that there have been losses, minor ones, since it is hard to believe that a story-loving age which appreciated Henryson would not have preserved a major work in one of its many collections. One attempt has been made to find the early poet. MacQueen suggests, more than tentatively, that two poems at the close of an up-dated 1489 copy of *Liber Pluscardensis* are his, one being a Scots translation requested by the late James II of a French lament for his sister the Dauphiness, who died in 1445, the other being a hard-hitting comparison of a Scots king's misgovernment to bad harping. The ascription is made because the first of these poems may have been in the original chronicle as commissioned by abbot Bothwell in 1461. It is, however, obviously written by a man of some age, and neither manner nor wording is at all Henrysonian. In the years when James, killed by an exploding canon in 1460, might have made the request Henryson was on the Continent. The chronicler, or copyist, it is amusing to note, excises eighteen stanzas as 'bot feinyit thing'. The second poem is published more fully in the Maitland collection and is explicitly written by someone close to the king who has his permission to criticise.[33] The king in question is plainly James III, as plainly the time is that of his final difficult years, and again the Henrysonian touch is missing.

I have no ascriptions to make that would partly supply the losses or remove the problem, but the cases of other Scots poets sketch some sort of explanation. In the decade after his leaving St Andrews in 1480 William Dunbar appears to have gone abroad, returned to be a minor secretary at court, and have travelled much in the king's service, as his *Flyting* 1491–92 and later poems testify, so that being only gradually noticed by his superiors he was only gradually given encouragement. The showy *Ballat Of Our Lady* assigns itself to his 'youth', 1. 59, *The Dance of The Sevin Deidly Sins* and two related poems give a date in 1491,[34] and it is my impression that *The Goldyn Targe*, which allegorizes a love affair, is an early exhibitionistic

bid for fame. It is about 1500 that his production begins to
become copious. He had then a chaplaincy and more
settled existence in a poem-demanding court. Sir David
Lindsay, who made his own poetical *début* about the same
age, that is, about thirty, assumes in a remark on the new
poet at the court of James V, John Bellenden, that without
'anctoritie', an established place, a poet will not have the
incentive to write much. Similarly he observes of the
dramatic poet James Inglis that the reward of a benefice,
the abbey of Culross, 'hes his pen maid impotent'. Luckily
for us Dunbar had provision without responsibility or
rustication.

With this in mind one remembers that Henryson had
been abroad for at least ten years, for two or three years
more in Scotland's west country—for all we know abroad
again for a period—and only on settling at the fairly
central and prestigious Dunfermline did he enjoy both
position and audience, but not of course at once. Dunfermline was not Edinburgh, and it may well have taken at
least a decade to make an impression on the occasionally
visiting court, and in his capacities as Master of the
Grammar School, lawyer and sometimes abbot's agent,
make his way into the company of Fife lairds and Edinburgh clerks who would applaud his genius, encourage his
verse. Even so his circumstances were never quite so
secular as those of Dunbar, and he would always have felt
the influence of the great abbey, and been involved in
functions that were all of a public and demanding kind.
He may indeed, just as the poetical evidence suggests,
have been in his early middle years when he composed the
Orpheus, and only have secured a wider attention when
about 1480 he began his topical and popular fables. The
simplest understanding of his mention of the patron who
suggested the *Aesop* to him as 'a noble Lord/Quhois name
as now it nedis not record' is that he expected the reader to
know him, his own Lord Abbot, at that time Henry
Crichton, who died in 1482.

Of course, the author of the *Testament* and *Robin and Makyne*, must once have written personal love poems, and known as does Orpheus how "Quhar luf gois on fors tornes the e", but at Dunfermline he would not have wanted the reputation of Dunbar's friend 'Merseir, Quha did in luf so lifly write'. As for any poems of piety that he wrote, the remmants, few as they are, are so various in their kinds, skills and effects, that losses can be assumed. However many, and in whatever form one cannot see discovery altering our picture of the poet or the man. He was essentially the philosophic observer and story-teller, not the kind of poet who finds his subject early. In the poems that we have he may take the stances of entertainer, social reformer, evangelist, but the prevailing impression made is that of the tragic and tragi-comic interpreter of life. I find it natural to imagine that he *found* himself when considering from many viewpoints the ineluctable passing of youth and its chances,

> "Robene, that warld is all away
> and quyte brocht till ane end",

or reflecting on both the physical and moral ironies of the experience of Orpheus and his lost Eurydice.

What there was in his life and temperament, outside the gift of the understanding imagination, that made him feel and express so poignantly the theme of human waste is, like so much else that the reader would wish to know, hidden from the biographer.

NOTES

1. Ms. Duncan has kindly shown me full copies made in the National Library. On Baron see note 23.
2. Concerning Moffat see *The Records of Dunfermline 1488–1584*, ed Erskine Beveridge, 1917. His comic poem of a husband and wife reversing working rôles is in the Bannatyne MS. (S.T.S.).

3. This was a Master Hary Henrison notary public, for a time convicted of 'heresy', perhaps when he gave up the priesthood for marriage (*Registrum Magni Sigilli*, III. 918, 2157, 2179; *The Protocol Book Of John Foular*, Scottish Record Society, vol. 2.

4. John Durkan, 'Education In The Century Of The Reformation' in *Essays On The Scottish Reformation 1513–1625*, ed. D. McRoberts, p. 167.

5. *Ibid.*

6. See Coutts (1909), Durkan (1977), respectively p. 47, p. 129.

7. *Liber Rectoris Universitatis*, no. 9, supplied to me by the Archivist. On the phrase *de mane legenti* see *Rashdall's Medieval Universities*, 1964, I, p. 438 f.

8. *Papal Registers*, xii. 297, under the year 1468.

9. *Liber Pluscardensis*, ed. F. J. H. Skene, I, 1877, xvi. Another copy was made in the Dunfermline scriptorium for William Schevez, archbishop of St Andrews 1478–96. Henryson quotes a Latin proverb from the fuller *Scotichronicon*, probably the Dunfermline copy, in the 'Parliament'.

10. The inquiries made by Ms. Duncan at almost all the universities that had been founded in Henryson's day have been unavailing.

11. *Liber Receptorum Nationis Alemanniae*, ed. Henri Dénifle, p. 35b.

12. *Rashdall's Medieval Universities*, 1964, I, pp. 438, 462–65.

13. Wood, *op. cit.*, xi, relying on Kinaston's 1639 statement that Henryson died 'very old', suggests 'some time early in the second quarter' of the century. MacQueen in *Scottish Society in the Fifteenth Century*, ed. J. M. Brown, p. 198, for no given reason proposes 'c. 1420–c. 1490'.

14. *Records Of the Privy Council*, II. 288.

15. On these Henrysons see William Stephen, *History of Inverkeithing and Rosyth*, 1920; entries in *The Protocol Book of James Young* (S.R.S.), *Exchequer Rolls, Registrum Magni Sigilli*.

16. Elphinston *senior's* love-lyric is in the Sheriff Clerk's Office, Aberdeen. I have deciphered it as a serious blending of Scots and Flemish, probably written at his university of Louvain about 1438. It is the earliest Scots lyric of its kind.

17. See *Burgh Records* under 'Plague'; James Grant *History of The Burgh Schools of Scotland*, 1876, p. 63.

18. Albert Herrmann, *The Taymouth Castle Manuscript Of Sir Gilbert Hay's Buik of Alexander the Conquerour*, Berlin, Gaertner, 1898. But the whole version is by an unknown hand whose colophon refers to Hay's 1438 version (Scottish Text Society).

19. *The Asloan Manuscript*, I (S.T.S.), pp. 297–8. Hay's *Buke of Knychthede* (S.T.S.) supplies the fictitious setting of an old man's narrative. The whole work is derivative, certainly using Henryson's poem.

20. For example, *Ratis Raving* (S.T.S.), 1570–71. The wolf in the 'Parliament' as an experienced chancellory clerk is also 'ane man of age'.
21. Quoted in full by W. Geddie, *Bibliography* (S.T.S.), xxxix.
22. Ranald Nicholson, *Scotland The Later Middle Ages*, 1974, p. 537.
23. *Ibid.*, pp. 500, 509, 520–1.
24. Montgomerie's *Dreme* is in the Maitland Society vols., 1836.
25. Nicholson, *op. cit.*, p. 505.
26. See my introduction to *Hary's Wallace* (S.T.S.), I. xiv–xxv.
27. Nicholson, *op. cit.*, p. 504, note 235. Sabbadino's contemporary account extolls her saintliness, disparages her husband.
28. Hary seems to have written much of the *Wallace* at Moonzie in Fife (S.T.S., liii).
29. MacQueen, *Robert Henryson The Major Narrative Poems*, p. 221.
30. *Ibid.*, pp. 189–99.
31. *Scottish Society in the Fifteenth Century*, ed. J. Brown, p. 204; J. MacQueen, 'Neoplatonism and Orphism in Fifteenth-Century Scotland', *Scottish Studies*, vol. 20, 1976, pp. 84–7.
32. Ebenezer Henderson, *Annals of Dunfermline*, 1879, p. 162; Nicholson, *op. cit.*, p. 471.
33. J. MacQueen in *Scottish Society* [etc.], p. 204. MacQueen does not mention the fuller, if still incomplete, version in the Maitland MS. which mentions the king's permission (Scottish Text Society, I, pp. 115–25).
34. The Shrove Tuesday to which the passage refers is that of 1491, not a later one as hitherto supposed. The related poems are *The Sowtar and Tailzouris War* and the *Amendis*.

CHAPTER II

THE TRADITION AND THE TIMES

Robert Henryson was born about the year of the death of the poet-king James I 1437, and died close to 1503 the year of the English marriage of James IV that was to be so fateful for Scotland. The greater part of his poetry was written in the unsettled reign of James III, 1460–1488. No doubt it was the Scotland of that unhappy king that most directly influenced the Henryson we meet in the poems, and a historian might be tempted to represent its more outstanding events and issues as their sufficient determining background. He would be encouraged to do so by the poet's patent criticism of that time in respect of the want of well enforced justice, his pictures of corrupt or indifferent churchmen, his prayers for a country reluctantly stirred to rebellion—till then more a feature of the English than the Scottish scene—the sheer intensity of his response to such evils: "Lord God, quhy sleipis Thow sa lang!".[1] It is likely, however, that as far as his awareness of the national tradition into which he was born is concerned, certain events previous to 1460 made a still deeper and more lasting impression, and even that no single reign of his lifetime was as important to him as the general difference between the Scotland of his age and that of the previous one as men imagined it.

In 1376–78 John Barbour, in his epic history of the Wars of Independence, was still able to describe the relationships of life in terms of simple loyalties to nation and church, to king and lord, within the family the bond of husband and wife. It is a national and therefore unquestioned system of what he call's 'dettis'. So much is it a single system that, he tells us, clerks dispute which should take priority, a man's debt to his wife or his debt to his lord. The point really is that all the basic bonds are familial. His assumed ideal is a national *communitas*, in which all sections, peasants included,—serfdom ceased in Barbour's lifetime and thanks to defensive wars and Celtic custom had never meant quite the same thing as it did in other countries—share a spirit of national and racial service. This, not an unqualified feudal hierarchy with a chivalric *ethos*, is the 'noble thing' that he calls 'fredome'.[2] And still in 1446, from his Scottish viewpoint, Richard Holland in his *Buik of the Howlat* could envisage all Europe as a family of nations and, with the reforming Council of Basle (1431–49) in mind, could imagine a Council of Europe attended by clergy and laity alike, by Pope, emperor, kings—among these 'his Serenite ever servable', the Scottish king—nobles and their following.[3] Again this is no mere assembly of the hierarchic powers. It is, according to the divinely made law of Nature who is personally present and consulted by all, a free coming together of the members of a family whose intimacy, happiness and harmony, are illustrated in the most homely ways: after a hymn to the Virgin, by music from many instruments, a pretended quarrel of clowns that ends in harmony, and a common feast. A pleasing if unrealistic picture, not so very far removed from the spirit of Augustine's *Civitas Dei*, and quite foreign, one would say, to the real medieval society of competitive interests, except that the young author clearly believes that something like it is possible, has witnessed the enthusiasm of the Conciliar and ecumenical movement, and has the still vivid Scottish memory of a genuinely national assertion of community that appealed to principles of natural law. Of course the poem ends appropriately with a picture of Holland's patrons, the earl and countess of Moray, flying together as doves in the original (but here very locally imagined) forest of love and happy growth that most people enter for shorter or longer periods in their lives.

But six years before the poetical fable was written an earl of Douglas had been murdered by the counsellors of the young James II of 'the fiery face', and the princes and nobles who had at first seen their advantage in supporting a reforming movement that challenged the Roman and Papal supremacy had already begun to view the Councils as equally dangerous to their authority. In conformity with the times, another earl of Douglas went splendidly attended to Rome in the Year of Jubilee 1450, to renew the religious allegiance that he had abandoned for Conciliarism and returned, within two years to be murdered, this time by the king himself. How much the family counted for is shown by the fact that the murderer did not yet dare to forfeit it. Three years later he attacked; Holland's patron, the new earl's twin brother, died in a confused skirmish, and the poet joined the earl in English exile. After many years of attempting to return to his native lands and country the ageing earl James was captured in a Border raid of 1484 and died a monkish prisoner in Lindores Abbey. He was still there in 1488 when James III, whose difficulties had come to a head, is said to have visited him and pointlessly asked for his aid and counsel. Henryson may have had occasion to visit the abbey, like his own of the Benedictine order, and in the same county, and seen the last of the 'Black' Douglases.[4]

In Holland's poem Christian realism enters with the judgement of Nature on the Houlat, which represents the rebellious self and is declared 'unamendable', and with the lament of that bird of darkness when the bright feathers that he has borrowed are stripped from him, "We cum pure, we gang pure, baith king and commoun"; and it may be said that in the poetry of Henryson, who had seen so much more of dissension in both Europe and Scotland than had Holland at the time of writing the *Buke*, it is this sense of the unamendable that dominates, the brighter part of Holland's vision being clouded and almost wholly obscured.

The destruction of the family, whose greatness derived from Robert Bruce, the memories of their exploits in Spain, at Danzig, Poiters, Otterburn, Baugé, Verneuil and Sark (1449), meant much more in Scotland than did the downfall of a king-making Warwick or Northumberland in England. It was not merely one more instance of the taming of baronial power by kings such as could be parallelled in other realms. It was not only a system of power that ended with it but a title, an array of battle honours almost synonymous with the national tradition. Of course, a lesser branch of the Douglas family rose under another title on the ruins of the greater, and many minor barons found wider scope for their ambitions. Boyds, Livingstones, Crichtons, Hepburns (made earls of Bothwell), Homes, sought to extend lands and power. Scottish kings had always ruled not by forces that they could themselves finance, but by the inherited prestige of an unchallenged line of descent, their sheer indispensability to the order, and the divisive diplomacy of 'divide and conquer' that fatally separated the Hamilton family from the Douglas. The fall of the Black Douglases clearly spelled the coming end of that order as Barbour and Holland had either known or been able to imagine it. It seemed to many that rôles had been reversed and that of the disruptive and predatory owl had been taken over by the king.

It is this sense of loss and division that makes the patriotic Hary who admired the Douglas record ('Bot sa mony as of Douglace has beyn/Gud of a kyn was nevir in Scotland seyn', XII. 1209–10), with an intention of tragic irony show a Stewart quarrel with Wallace at Falkirk and so lose the day to our 'auld enemies', and in his quarrelling actually accuse the great patriot of being the owl in the fable (XI. 99–144). When James III sought to strengthen his position with a policy of English

marriages, 'the inbringing of Inglismen' as a rebel parliament was to call it, he acted according to the alien logic of
the power game of Lancastrian and Yorkist rulers in
England who had turned to France and Burgundy for
help, and so introduced yet more division; when he set
himself up as a rival to his land-hungry lords and lairds in
the acquisition of estates and rents he might again seem to
be doing the sensible thing from the viewpoint of an exchequer that was always ill provided, but inevitably he
alienated his people; when he delayed or intervened in
church appointments—Henryson's own abbot Crichton
transferred from Paisley against the wishes of the monks
had been such a case[5]—he made enemies in the most basic
of national institutions. The ancient image of kingship,
which had never been the same in Scotland as elsewhere,
being more that of popular leadership than autocratic
monarchy, was tarnished.[6] Naturally the author of the
Lancelot translation, which keeps up an intermittent commentary on the contemporary scene, saw his death as that
of 'a verray wretch', a mere hoarder of wealth.[7] The
commons, the estate most reluctant to question the old
loyalties, saw him, according to Henryson's 'Lyoun and
the Mous', sleeping in his office, neglectful of his dignity
and duties as Guardian and First Justiciar of the realm.

Yet the character or peculiar conduct of any one of the
Jameses was not the deciding factor in the new situation,
important at a given moment as it might be. It was inevitable then, as now, that there should be an accelerating
movement of wealth and power to the centre, with it a
growing criticism of and cynicism about the centre, a
sense of communal loss. The kingdom could never have
been the harmony desiderated by Barbour, Holland,
Hary, the author of the 'harp poem' and the chroniclers,
as they partly supposed it to have been in the good old
days, but no class, least of all the clerical intelligentsia,
enjoyed seeing it so rudely violated. James IV, the most
likable, popular and effective, of all the Stewarts brought

back much of the lost unity simply by doing the traditional things (alongside the new), getting to know his country in all its sheriffdoms and classes, attending justice ayres, cultivating the noble families (who were happy to supply him with mistresses), being conspicuously pious, showing a liking for combat, having the right attitude to England, being seen in his ship-building and collection of artillery, and intervention in the politics of Europe, to make not only himself but his country great. It is symptomatic of the restored national sentiment that bishop Elphinston issued the first liturgy of Scottish saints 1509–10. The high, confident colouring of Dunbar's courtly confections and religious celebrations, like the profuse energy of Douglas's descriptions in *The Palyce of Honour*, dedicated to James, are responses to a prince who could supply the inspiration and leadership that was expected of him. It was as if all parties collaborated in the pretence that no great change had occurred, that what was in process was a restoration and not a revolution.

The fourth James knew better. He pursued successfully the powers in state and church that his father had vainly sought, sometimes treating the patrimony of the church as if it were his own, significantly protecting heretics and choosing Erasmus to be his son's tutor. And his court-poet Dunbar knew better. It has been too easily assumed that his reference to the wind that 'Dryvis in the see of Loller-dry that blawis' meant little, and that his complaint of the preference of the new to the old in the scheme of promotions, of the upstart to the nobly born, the hearing given at court to the sellers of novelties in merchandise, doctoring, printing, transmutation of metals to gold, even the secret of flight, are the mere grumblings of an envious place-seeker. A morbidity and cynicism that protested against the bright surface of things, to which he himself necessarily responded, are evident in his best verse. They may seem small things but meant more, that the king enjoyed equally an old-style tournament and the farcical parody of the same, and that it is *The Dance of the Sevin Deidly Sinnis* that precedes one of these parodies as reported by Dunbar. The old order that rebelled in the reign of Henryson's James III and kept up some of its appearances under James IV was in haste to become a new order, and until it did only acted a part in which it could no longer wholly believe.

This last phenomenon has been observed in other countries by many historians, Burckhardt and De Sanctis in their histories of Italian culture,[8] Huizinga in his *Waning of the Middle Ages*, noticing striking contrasts and contradictory extremes of behaviour, particularly a display or *étallage* of piety that is strenuous or costly but implies no practical respect for the church. In Scotland kings, nobles and burgesses, founded chaplainries, or corporations known as collegiate churches, for the purpose of having masses said for the souls of the founders and their kin, but did nothing to urge churchmen back to their pastoral and preaching duties. Relics were much sought after; in this half of the century the burgesses of Edinburgh thought it worthwhile to secure the arm-bone of the saint after whom their church of St. Giles was named; in 1490 archbishop Schevez searched at Fordoun in Angus for the bones of St. Palladius, reputed to have brought Christianity to Scotland in the fifth century. Men who had no zeal for reform crusaded or went on pilgrimage: Scots fought at Rhodes against the Turk, James III and James IV considered leading a crusade, the former receiving the sword now in the Scots regalia, both kings being devoutly frequent pilgrims at home, though their devotions did not move them to respect the integrity of the church. James III, as noticed, condoned the sale of the teinds of Stirling parish by his appointee, Henryson's abbot, to pay for his nomination.[9] James IV did regular penance at Dunfermline or his new-built house of Franciscan Observantines, but he made his brother, next his illegitimate son, archbishop of St Andrews. Of course the alliance of acquisitive politics with superstitious, since impractical, piety could be parallelled in the France of Louis XI and the Italy of Pope Julius II.

In Italy, De Sanctis observes, everyone worshipped and no one believed. The one fresh, honest statement of faith in Pulci's *Morgante Maggiore* 1491 is the credo of the dwarf giant Margutte, "nel buon vino ho fede/E credo che sia salvo chi gli crede' (I believe in good wine and that a man is saved who believes in it", XVII. st. 115), a comfortable doctrine shared by Dunbar's Master Andrew Kennedy who committed his soul 'Into my lordis wyne cellar', and not unlike the happy opinion of Henryson's newly dined fox that when one had a full belly then was the time to die, which he promptly did. Italian society in De Sanctis' phrase, was 'licenziosa e burlevole', self-indulgent and trifling, its finest verse caring only for delightful externals, as do the *Orfeo* and *Stanze* of Poliziano. In poetry a strangely trivial Europe but for the significant exceptions: France, thanks to Villon, fetching a real voice from the low life of Paris; Spain pronouncing the most impressive of funeral incantations in the *Coplas* of Jorge Manrique. For England's untiring Lydgate Shakespeare's words will do, "Goodman Dull, thou hast spoken all this time and said nothing".

The same European society does seem to have believed very sincerely and anxiously in death and hell. The death-dance and the *memento mori* in macabre forms went every-where, hence an exceptional morbidity and somewhat escapist emotionalism in its abundant devotional literature. When a Scots writer of about 1500, describes the Virgin Mary as both pirate and safe port of souls one may be intrigued by the anticipation of Donne's violent imagery, 'And ne'er be chaste except you ravish me', but the effect is merely one of extravagance. Equally such prolonged acts of piety as *The Passioun of Christ* by Walter Kennedy (the flyter with Dunbar) and the popular *Contemplacioun of Synnaris* (soon printed in London) by

William Touris, both authors intent on a harrowing blow-by-blow account of suffering, do more for themselves than the reader.[10] Nor are Henryson and Dunbar wholly exempt from this spiritual masochism, though they do it better; an apparently old Henryson writes his shocking *Three Powis* (skulls) and Dunbar writes his almost song-like *Passion*.

The most ambitious poem of the period is Hary's epic *Wallace* (1475–76)[11]. Its hero loves and hates in the extremest fashion, has an unexpected variety of moods, and tendency to 'braith (angry) teris', moving between passionate commitment and a despondency in which 'he seis the warld sa full of fantasie'. His death is, of course, a martyrdom that moves the poet so much that he chooses to 'lightly pass' over the still more terrible details that history provided. Hary's poem is interesting not only for its characterisation. Its author knows his contemporary world that is moving away from, has moved away from, the heroic scene and its values. When in the first lines of his epic he complains 'We . . . haldis us euir till uthir business', it is more than James III's English policy that he has in mind. Wallace, watching Bruce see his advantage on the English side, exclaims 'the warld is contrar-lik'. The traitor Menteith, a Stewart, has been particularly the hero's comrade and is genuinely concerned for the souls imperilled by war but it is English gold that decides his treachery. He reflects at last, "till thrifty men it dois full mekill scaith". One thinks of "This yellow slave will knit and break religions", the exclamation of Shakespeare's Timon of Athens (IV. iii. 33–4). King, nobles, bishops, were ready to engage in trade on their own account, and nobles, though insincerely, accepted English pensions. Significantly, in Henryson's 'Parliament' the independently minded mare will not go to court, and his country mouse foreswears the dubious pleasures of the town. The questioning melancholy that accompanied the new prosperity shows everywhere;

Dunbar may often use the most brilliant and positive colours, as in *The Thrissil and the Rose* and the 'magnificat' of his Resurrection poem, and he may be as benefice-hungry as others, but he is most the poet and most himself in the saddest lines—

> Quhy will thow hald that will away,
> Or craif that thow may have mo space,
> Thow tending to ane uther place,
> A journay going everie day?

Perhaps this questioning sadness has a place in the showy piety of the time, a piety that knows how little basis it has in the ordinary affairs of life. Poetically a golden age for Scotland, and partly because, as with Elizabethan England, it was one in which the splendid promises were unsettling. Henryson and Dunbar would have understood that the melancholy Jacques spoke for much of Shakespeare. It is not so unnatural that tragic poets appear in such times of promise and disillusionment, or indeed that they should produce a poet who is great in both the comic and the tragic faculties.

Italy, the intellectual centre of Europe, was exploring the Humanist sources and ideas that would soon, as Burckhardt says, give the idea of culture an almost religious fervour, from the first suggesting a possible division between it and the Christian tradition, a division that is already apparent in Pulci's creation of the expository devil Astarotte and will soon be clear in the mock-heroic paganism of Ariosto's *Orlando Furioso*, 1513–15. Sir Thomas More's Augustinian *Utopia* of about the same time is one illustration of how differently the northern mind then responded to the promise of a renaissance. In Scotland the Christian and national traditions were at least alive enough to make the best minds aware of what they were in danger of losing, and serious enough about the loss to make a profound response. It may be argued that Scotland was merely more backward, less progressive, but the fact remains that in the last quarter of the century its poetical response was the most considerable that Europe had to offer, particularly from one man of genius who was moved by the time's dilemma to look beyond the present scene to the human scene as it would always be.

It is a convention in any comment on national culture at this period, to rate it by the evidences of the Humanist impulse, noticing the affectation of a Ciceronian Latin, much more important the inspiration of classical imagining in literature, the effect of classical thinking about the various kinds of relationship between state and citizen, the educationist drive resulting therefrom. What can be said is that Europe had a new stimulus to move along paths it had already taken. The latest renaissance had other and more immediate sources of excitement than ancient authors. And one should observe that in the closing decades of the century it was not the countries where Humanist activity was greatest that produced the most meaningful literature.

None the less, the Humanist phenomena are plain in Scotland. As early as 1446–49 the chronicler Walter Bower digresses on Aristotle's *Ethics, Politics* and, more surprisingly, on the theory of 'imitation' expounded in his *Poetics*.[12] The secretaries of James III and James IV, Archibald Whitelaw and Patrick Paniter, wrote an epistolary style not unworthy of later and more famous Scots Latinists like Florence Wilson and George Buchanan. That the new studies should accelerate the use of Latin-type words such as MacQueen notices in Henryson is not surprising, but the tendency is already apparent in *The Kingis Quair* (c. 1435), and had French examples that need not be labelled 'renaissance'. In the matter of education there were important initiatives: an Act of 1496 that directed the sons of barons to legal study for the better execution of justice had in view the facilities of the three universities, two of them founded quite recently, those of Glasgow (1451) and Aberdeen (1495). It was in Greek and rhetoric that Erasmus briefly tutored James IV's short-lived son Alexander at Sienna, and it is said by Dempster that Henry abbot of Kelso corresponded with Poliziano.[13] Certainly Gavin Douglas was interested in the Roman festivals of the Humanist Pomponio Laeto, and himself followed Annibale Caro with the translation of Virgil's *Aeneid* that is still the most alive of all such attempts.

There is no reason to suppose that Henryson knew Greek, yet his allusions to the Greek myths cannot be fully traced to the usual textbooks, Fulgentius or the *Genealogie Deorum*. His interest in them is clearly a poet's as well as a teacher's. The muses, Plato's soul of the world, the celestial harmony 'passing all instrumentis musicall', and others, usually are brought in with a didactic relevance, but in *The Testament of Cresseid* for once we catch him out in a purely self-indulgent digression on the four horses of the sun.

The fact of Humanist influences is interesting, but it is fortunate that the spirit and culture of the nation remained basically true to tradition. A novel and bright inspiration had begun to be experienced but older ideals had not been abandoned, only furthered by it. The popular direction of Scottish attitudes to government and education may be reinforced by the new spirit but does not derive from it. When Hary creates the great figure of Wallace as he is still known today, his only debt to the *Aeneid* is its example of a well organised whole, conveniently in twelve Books. When Douglas says that he wants 'onletterit folk' as well as 'clerkis' to memorise and recite his *Eneados*, he is sincere because he has a precedent in their knowledge of the stories of Bruce and Wallace.[14] Douglas and Henryson do not get their feeling for the hardships of the labourer's lot from the classics. What makes the Scots poetical world real is its creators' habit of *application* of their reading to the society and scene they know. It has been inanely objected to Douglas that he can speak of the Bacchantes as 'Bacchus nuns', and see *pius Aeneas* as the type of responsible leadership that any kingdom, particularly his Scotland, desiderates. Similarly, when Henryson in his *Orpheus* cites Aristotle's *Rhetoric* on the function of education, to make raw youth 'in all vertues excellent', it is a strictly Christian interpretation that he gives. Aeneas is said in the Prologue to have 'everie vertu belangand a gentill knicht', a very practical mixture of the Roman and the contemporary. What is assumed here is that the hero is like Virgil himself, not so odd an assumption, and one that agrees perfectly with the ideal enunciated by Sir Gilbert Hay in 1456 of the 'knycht clerk', Sir Gilbert being himself a worthy example.[15] The same ideal is the whole point of Henryson's opening discourse in the *Orpheus*, on the absurdity of having uneducated men in positions of power. One may even go so far as to say that whatever corruption existed in church and state—and Douglas furthered his own and his House's interests when after Flodden he counselled his nephew, the Governor—the Scots poets of the period had as convinced and as austere an *ideal* of the unity of doctrine and practice as prevailed in the subsequent age of Calvinism.

The belief in application, as against the shadow that Walter Bower calls *nomen sine re*, is traditional, and its relative vocal earnestness beside the literary voice in Italy and France goes a long way towards explaining the more serious attention required by the Scottish poets, particularly Henryson. It also helps to explain that already mentioned theme of 'human waste', in both the worldly and otherworldly senses of the phrase, the melding of Christian principle with recognition of a very human, and therefore necessarily imperfect, even hostile, society sharpening the poet's sympathy with inevitable moral and physical catastrophe.

I have spoken of a 'popular' or patriarchal direction in

Scottish notions of government.[16] This oddity is as old as, or older than, the Declaration of Independence 1320, and cannot be stressed enough. It would persist, so far as expectations went, into the age of the union of crowns if not nations in 1603, and would be frustrated by it. Obviously it relates to John Barbour's pregnant description of his countrymen, 'the few folk of ane symple land'. James III's fatal mistake in preferring to govern at a remove from his subjects has been noticed. It was not merely a convention that chroniclers should invariably, if misleadingly, say of every other dead king and Guardian that he was the comforter of the widow, the support of the orphan, the humble, the distressed, and so forth. He had at least to make a show of speaking familiarly with, listening to the complaints of, ordinary men. He should strive to be remembered as 'good king' so and so. When in his *Satire of The Three Estates* acted before James V and Marie de Lorraine Lindsay made a character declaim, "What is a king? Nocht but an officer", he merely stated what every Scottish king had to hear or read. Nor was this popular tradition of duties to be performed and rights to be respected confined to men of education and the smaller or greater gentry. Barbour could say that it was willing ploughmen, given leadership, who had won the war of independence, since only free men, he insists grandly (with a reference to Scipio's freeing the slaves of Rome in time of peril), can fight well for freedom. Froissart tells us of the surprise of French captains in late fourteenth-century Scotland on encountering the violent and successful resistance of peasants to arbitrary foraging and billeting. Bower relates with relish that he watched a butcher stop King Robert (father of James I) riding away without settling accounts; and fifteen years after Henryson's death the historian John Mair, a farmer's son, observes with approval that a peasant would return a noble's blow with interest; and he asserts as a truism, 'A king does not own his kingdom as a man owns his shirt', a saying which, of course, equally applied to the relationship of landlord and tenant, of churchman and layman.

What underlies this popularism in a none the less feudal society that still related much more to the countryside than the town, is not only Barbour's factual observation, or the influence of a mostly people-derived priesthood, but the cult of kinship in a society still of mainly Celtic composition, often a source of conflict but issuing in a genuine sense of national community. One can notice the assumed unity that overrides the momentary divisions in these simple lines of the great ballad—its author knew Froissart's account—describing the Douglas's invasion of England and victory at Otterburn:

> He chose the Gordons and the Graemes,
> With them the Lindsays light and gay,
> But the Jardines wouldna with him ride
> And they rue it to this day.

It is this sense of community that explains the sympathy that the schoolmaster Robert Henryson has for the labourer's privations, 'half ane purgatory', and the noble-born Douglas's feeling in the scene that prefaces the sixth Book of his *Eneados*, for the 'little herd grume' out in the worst of winter weathers.

This spirit is made so much of here because it connects closely with the familiar, down-to-earth understanding that Henryson has of his Aesopic world of very ordinary human beasts, their needs and greeds and their defeats, and the sense of a shared situation that it conveys. And connects also with the presentation of his King Orpheus, homely and familial and none the less kingly for that, who finds that his natural way is not through the heavens but by a (very Scottish) moor that leads by such 'redy wayis', past figures of suffering, to the inevitable test and failure; with the Christ-like Swallow's care for the more heedless birds who are doomed by the simple handicap of ever oncoming necessity; and with the Cresseid who very naturally could not think that 'all cummis for the best'.

Henryson's created world is not that of Chaucer's mostly prosperous and well entertained pilgrims—his Parson and the latter's peasant brother do not really belong with these holiday-makers—exuberant within their strictly typical relationships, their stories conveniently suited to the teller's social standing or function; nor is it that of the renaissance gentleman or prince romanticized or philosophized by great bourgeois poets like Spenser or Shakespeare. Being Scottish its significance is not attached so patently to category and class. After all, his intention is to show, very barely, how all men are what they are, according to Jonathan Swift's reminder but very differently felt, 'not *animale rationale* but *animale rationis capax*,' a capacity that their nature and needs do not allow them to exercise as they should.

It has been suggested that Henryson wrote different kinds and styles of poetry for different audiences, the *Fabillis* for 'a middle-class professional audience of private readers . . . predominantly masculine', the *Testament* for 'a more courtly audience with more feminine interests'.[17] It is not a helpful suggestion. For which audience was *Orpheus* or *Robene and Makyne* intended? The distinction is modern and misleading in so far as it tends to define and limit the character and appeal of his verse. Plainly he wrote for himself and anyone who would read and listen, speaking out of a tradition that lived by verities that were at once its own and universal, perhaps best appreciated by 'clerks' but substantially apprehended by man and woman, educated and uneducated Scot, alike.[18]

NOTES

1. 'The Taill of the Scheip and the Doig', 1295.
2. See my introduction to the forthcoming edition of the *Bruce*, Scottish Text Society.

3. M. P. McDiarmid, 'Richard Holland's *Buke of the Howlat*: An Interpretation' in *Medium Aevum*, ed. J. A. W. Bennett, vol. xxxviii, 1969, no. 3. The text is in *Scottish Alliterative Poems*, ed. F. J. Amours, S.T.S. A new text is being prepared by Felicity Riddy of Stirling University.

4. The factually authoritative account of the reign of James II is that of A. I. Dunlop, *The Life and Times of James Kennedy Bishop of St Andrews*, 1950, but she has the centralist bias: progressive kings, reactionary barons, etc. See Ranald Nicholson, *op.cit.*

5. Nicholson, *op. cit.*, pp. 458–9.

6. See my essay 'The Kingship of the Scots in their Writers', *Scottish Literary Journal*, May 1979, vol. 6, no. 1. This gives much of the evidence for the view of the 'tradition' given here.

7. The author makes much use of Sir Gilbert Hay's 1456 *Buke of Knychthede*, and *Buke of the Governance of Princes*. For the phrase quoted see 1. 1806 in the S.T.S. edition of M. M. Gray, 1912.

8. Jacob Burckhardt, *The Civilization Of The Renaissance*, trans. L. Goldscheider, 1944; Franceso de Sanctis, *Storia Della Letteratura Italiana*, ed. Benedetto Croce, vol. 1, 1939, chs. 11, 12. This is perhaps the greatest of all literary histories.

9. See Chapter I, note 32.

10. For the 'pirate' comparison and poems see *Devotional Pieces In Verse And Prose*, ed. J. A. W. Bennett, Scottish Text Society, 1955, pp. 281, 7, 64.

11. See my edition and introduction already cited.

12. On the reference to Aristotle's '*poetria*' and doctrine of imitation see *Scotichronicon*, Book I, ch. 35.

13. Thomas Dempster. *Historia Ecclesiastica*, but I have been unable to trace Henry's correspondence, if such existed.

14. *Eneados*, ed. D. Coldwell, S.T.S., vol. 4, 1960, p. 193. Priscilla Bawcutt explores his 'Library' in *Bards and Makaris*, pp. 107–26.

15. *The Buke of Knychthede*, ed. J. H. Stevenson. S.T.S., 1914, p. 23. Sir Gilbert, former chamberlain of Charles VI of France, has a fine contempt for superstition, witchcraft, astrology (as had John Barbour) and preaches 'science of clergy to know the lawis' to all gentry, an ideal enforced in Scotland by the education act of 1496. The foundation of universities is a duty of princes urged by Haye.

16. For a fuller treatment of this topic see the reference in note 6 to my article.

17. John MacQueen, 'The literature of fifteenth-century Scotland' in *Scottish Society in the Fifteenth Century*, p. 205.

18. The most recent edition is by Denton Fox, Oxford, Clarendon Press, 1981. That of Charles Elliott, Oxford, 1974, is preferred here.

CHAPTER III

ORPHEUS AND EURYDICE

Almost certainly it was in *The Tale of Orpheus And Erudices His Quene* that as poet Henryson found himself, that is, found what his experience had to say and how it wanted him to say it, his meaning becoming explicit with the form that his story-telling developed, and the individual response that it seemed to demand from him. The tale of Orpheus offered itself to the poet in already stated outlines and with an already accepted interpretation. Greek in origin and mentioned by Virgil and Ovid,[1] it was none the less best known to Christian Europe in the moralized version that Boethius gives in his *De Consolatione Philosophiae*, Lib. III, Metrum XII, and in Henryson's time in the allegorizing commentaries of Guillaume de Conches, Nicholas Trivet (the poet's special mentor) and Denys the Carthusian, all of which he seems to have consulted.[2] He would not have wished to differ from their analyses or been conscious of the difference of meaning that he does introduce. He agrees with their didactic exposition of a spiritual failure but transforms this with a tragic poet's awareness of 'the pity of it'. Every man loses his Eurydice, his aspiration, inescapably; 'Than perfyte resoun wepis wounder saire' (445), and not only the 'perfyte resoun' in him but the hurt human being who cannot help being what he is, imperfect and vulnerable.

To appreciate Henryson's characteristic interpretation of the great myth it helps to notice conceptions and treatments of Orpheus that were advanced in the particular moral tradition within which he worked. The main themes of the Greek imagination prevailed though they

were given a Christian gloss. To Pindar Orpheus was 'the
father of songs', the inventor of music and poetry. He had
therefore in him something of the divine, for to the Greeks,
as to their poetical and philosophical successors, harmony
seemed a significant attribute of the created world. It was
to be seen and, Plato fancied, intellectually heard in the
ordered movements of the heavenly bodies—a fancy that
Henryson alludes to when he mentions Plato's notion of
the world having a soul (219–25).[3] The same divine music
was more physically known to man, indeed capable of
description according to Macrobius and Boethius, and
Henryson lists some of the terms of their analysis.[4] In 'The
Preiching of the Swallow', where he asserts that 'God in
all his werkis witty is', he notices another illustration of
this divine 'wit' or intellectual harmony, the order and
mutual support that the seasons display. Doubtless he
remembers Boethius's observation in his treatise on
music, 'Each season bears its own fruits or helps the others
to bear theirs',[5] thus springtime is said in the *Preiching* to
be 'the Secretar off somer with his seill' (1707).

The idea of a divine harmony or order in creation
inevitably demands consideration of the apparent
dissonances, the unhappy discords of actual experience as
they present themselves in both the inner and outer worlds
of man, the forces that Boethius represents by Fortune
and her wheel. These should be reconciled in the peace of
the good life and its understanding, or not understanding,
faith, when

> the gret sollicitud,
> Quhile up, quhile down, to wyn this warldis gud,
> Cessis furthwith, and our complexioun
> Waxis quyet in contemplacioun. (515–18)

So Denys, who is remembered here,[6] had maintained, but
this is precisely what Henryson finds so difficult to
achieve, as his *Prayer For the Pest*, which is at moments an
argument with God, makes very clear, for example, 'Our

deid [death] may nathing our synnys recompens'. The dubious hope in Calchas's comforting of Cresseid dismissed from Diomede's bed, "Peraventure all cummis for the best", speaks the same disquiet. At a level beyond doctrine Henryson does not believe. The moralists to whom he had turned for an interpretation do not admit to the same difficulties, and seem to think that they have said all when they have given each related event its orthodox gloss; though it may be thought that Guillaume's distrust of the poet as one who 'wounds and betrays' rather than 'guides and consoles' shows that he might have understood, even if he disapproved of, a response like Henryson's. In brief, the brilliantly articulate restatement of 'catharsis' that has been quoted above defines an ideal state of mind that the poet considers to be rarely, if at all, available to human nature.

If it seems improbable to anyone—especially someone who like E. M. Tillyard supposes that the hierarchical scheme of things presented by artists as various as Dante and Dürer spoke unexceptionably for feeling as well as faith—that a late fifteenth-century poet should respond to experience in any but an affirmatively orthodox manner, let it be remembered that the unrest of Conciliar thinking about church government and doctrine was still abroad and had not disappeared with the Councils, was indeed active in the Scottish universities, that in a decade or two royal authority in Scotland would even show itself tolerant of the heretic,[7] and that to a poet like William Dunbar cosmic order was indifferently apt for hymnic or farcical purposes. What would Dante, who damned Ulysses for seeking to go beyond the bounds of nature, have said of the Scots abbot who attempted to win the secret of flight? Perhaps just as important, it should also be remembered, as it so rarely is, how the supposedly Christian Boethius had presented Orpheus,

> Inmites superos querens
> Infernos adiit domos.

In that accusation as it is developed by Henryson is the precedent for the blasphemy of Cresseid who finds what it means 'to mufe and steir our craibit [malicious] goddis'. Boethius and his commentators simply record the complaint as the first instance, no different from the last when for a second time he loses his wife, of his reprehensible subjection to earthly attachments. The complaint is seen as ordinary human weakness in one of its many irrational reactions to stress, to be duly punished. It is Henryson alone, without rejecting the Boethian meaning, who makes the response take an aggressive form, and persistently adopts the attitude of pity, showing it in Orpheus himself.

Thus at the news of Eurydice's rape by death he does not simply go *querens*, lamenting (120–23):

> This noble king inflammit all in ire
> And rampand as ane lyoun ravenus,
> With awfull luke and eyne glowand as fyre,
> Speris the maner.

This is the lion-king as Scots poets and their national standard depict him, as Dunbar depicts him in *The Thrissil and the Rois*, 'Quhois noble yre is *parcere prostratis*' but *debellare superbos*. The grief is not passive but angry and passionate, 'The bludy teris sprang out of his eyne' (150). There is even the tinge of rebellion when he finds that he can bring music to his harp no longer, cannot be consoled, and abandons the world, "My wikit werd [malicious fate] in wildernes to waire" [spend] (156). Finally there is the direct charge of injustice done by "my faire fader Phebus" against his "awne sone Orpheus", "thi barne and child". Let no one stop his search, "for seike her suth I sall,/And nother stynt nor stand for stok nor stone". Eurydice was taken "withoutin gilt begild". He cannot and does not accept the will of heaven. At least in accordance with this, different in degree of guilt as the cases are, is the poet's reminder to the reader of Cresseid's story that she had Fortune to contend with, and whatever her faults there can be no occasion for her reputation 'throw wickit langage to be spilt [injured]'. When one remembers that in late medieval and renaissance symbolism Phoebus, the sun, commonly represented God, and Orpheus was a name for the son of God, the doctrinal import of the charge of injustice will be fully appreciated. Gavin Douglas in his *Eneados*, 459–70, addressing the Virgin Mary, is at pains as a poet to say his allegiance is to her and not to Orpheus's mother, the Muse Calliope, yet in the first of the lines now to be quoted takes over verbally Henryson's description of the nursing Calliope (69–70), and proceeds to the above-mentioned identification,

> For the sweit liquor of thy pappis quhite
> Fosterit that Prynce, that hevynly Orpheus,
> Ground of all gude, our Salvyour Ihesus.

That Henryson is setting himself up covertly, or Orpheus explicitly, as a doctrinal rebel against the Will of Heaven is not to be imagined. For a moment, however, the puzzling cry of Christ upon his cross has been echoed, "My God, my God, why hast thou forsaken me?;"[8] and by indulging the feelings that always went with his favourite theme of injustice he has allowed the sufferer a stronger voice of religious protest than had been heard in European literature before. He thus gives to the hero's experience the dimension of fundamental questioning that is required in any truly tragic treatment. In the course of Shakespeare's *King Lear* the Boethian principle is stated, "bear free and patient thoughts", but the play is great tragedy because Lear cannot, is not allowed to do so, and is made to utter his sense of the injustice of things with unequalled power. It is in that direction, the vocalizing of the hero's difficulties, that Henryson moves, neither more nor less orthodox than his great successor, and asking the same distressful questions. Before him his royal countryman James Stewart in *The Kingis Quair*, and a little after

the *Orpheus* Hary in the tragic epic *Wallace*, voiced the
same questions less intensely,[9] allowing events, James's
happy marriage and liberation, Scotland's ultimate
independence, to answer for them. That they did voice
them with some power—I find it impossible to recognise
any such sincere voice in Chaucer's 'tragedie' of Troilus—
is mentioned here only to remark on a native context of
concern with, and writing on, the central tragic issue that
is not to be found elsewhere at this time.

Scottish thinking about literature, as about society,
developed along traditional lines. It was predominantly
religious in its *dicta* on the matter, purpose and methods,
of writing. It was at the same time much concerned with
the realities of experience. John Barbour in his *Bruce*
(1376–78) and Andrew Wyntoun in his *Orygynal Chronicle*
(c. 1405–20) had naturally stressed the importance of
'suthfastness', truth of matter, and had rejected merely
chivalric ways of representing their heroes. The same
value informs their dignified but quite undecorative
'carpyng' (Barbour's term) or style. And this belief in
letting good matter have its own voice can be appreciated
in the masterly saint's life known as *Mary the Egypciane* (c.
1400),[10] so much more impressive than Chaucer's pious
confection, *The Prioresses Tale*. In the fifteenth century
it is interesting to watch how the incoming complication of
styles, and temptation to indulge a merely literary
rhetoric, is controlled by the taste for simplicity and real
voices that the poets had inherited. This is not the place to
illustrate this continuing characteristic of Scottish verse
but its relation to the religious preoccupation in poetry
will be understood.

Even Gavin Douglas's practical observation in his
Prologue on how to read poetry, 'weill at a [one] blink sle
[sophisticated] poetry not tane is', refers mainly to
ramifications of meaning, and his sensible comments on
the art of poetical translation are similarly directed: in the
case of the *Aeneid* language must not alienate but make

attractively human the good man and good governor. Walter Bower in his *Scotichronicon* (1446–49) refers to Aristotle's recognition that imitation gives pleasure, only to warn against incitement to excessive grief.[11] And in his *Meroure of Wisdome* the theologian John Ireland, a Fife man who would be well known to Henryson, confines tragedy to the business of showing 'in the begynning gret plesaunce And in the ende all manere of sorow and displesaunce', because relatively life is 'a maner of hell'.[12] The latter phrase may exemplify those extremes of feeling that Huizinga finds characteristic of the century, but it also recalls Matthew Arnold's observation that to the Greek tragedians life was a hell. Certainly such extreme views favour the tragic vision because they encourage the intense sympathies and intense expression that a writer in this kind must display. When the poet writes in his *Moralitas* 571–72,

> Bot Orpheus has wone Erudices
> Quhen our desyre with resoun makis pes

he sketches the ideal harmony that he does not expect his hero or any man more than momentarily to enjoy. Herein lies the tragic impression made by Orpheus. As his failure is treated it reflects a total view of life, equally applicable to the working-men whose life Henryson sees to be 'half ane purgatory', just as Lear's sense of personal injustice extends to the 'poor naked wretches' he learns to pity.

The relationship of the *Orpheus* to the traditional and conservative aspects of the cultural situation into which Henryson was born should be evident. It should be equally evident that it is the fusion of conservative mould and new informing spirit that gives his genius its opportunity. The recent stress on recognisably Humanistic elements in his thinking about the classical myth has been overdone, and so far as it isolates these is misleading; the assertion of MacQueen, for example, that 'The poem in fact is constructed on Neoplatonic [Ficinian] principles to illustrate Neoplatonic doctrine',[13] however interesting its references to sources of that doctrine may be, is convincing only as it takes account of the Platonism that had long since been diffused into western thought by early and well known authors like Boethius, Macrobius and Chalcidius. A direct influence from the Florentine classicist Marsilio Ficino is out of the question, and the description of the poem's general intention in Ficinian terms seems to me as trivialising as it is mistaken. As the same critic recognises, the *Favola di Orfeo* of Poliziano is itself much less neo-Platonic than the *Orpheus* as interpreted by him. Neo-Platonism, with its characteristic depreciation of the material *nexus* of life and spirit was to provide a language for some of the more optimistic and 'escapist' educational fancies of Spenser, Milton and Shelley, even of Wordsworth, but fortunately these poets have more substantial matter in their thought to recommend them. Certainly it was not a philosophy that was likely to appeal to the experience, morals and beliefs, of the practical Scot. Henryson is no 'ineffectual angel fluttering in the void his luminous wings in vain'.

Scholastic commentary, pedantic as it is, has the discipline of logic and, more important, the basically human relevance, the realism, that is wanting to Ficino and his ilk, and it will be useful to the reader to have in view the intellectual shape of Orpheus's experience as that 'noble theologe', Master Nicholas Trivet, chose to see it, along with some few suggestions of the preceding Guillaume and subsequent Denys. The further contribution of Boccaccio can then be considered.

Orpheus, being the son of Phoebus and the Muse Calliope is, or represents, according to Trivet, reason endowed with eloquence. His wife Eurydice is the 'affective' or feeling part of man's nature, more to the point, she is man's desiring, that reason would make one with itself. Briefly reason wins this Eurydice, but in the pleasant field of life, when the will to virtue which is figured by the herdsman Aristaeus, would possess her, she flees, and is mortally stung by the lurking serpent of this attractively sensual world, and in that respect finds death and hell. To win back to heavenly things his desire, the lost Eurydice, Orpheus plays the music of reason, which is harmony with the upper world, and should overcome the hell of fleshly desire. Seeking her in this hell he must first conquer the three-headed monster Cerberus, which is mortal sin as it menaces childhood, youth and age alike, wonderful as each of these may find divine knowledge. Next there are the three Furies to subdue, Allecto, Thesiphone, Megera, who are evil working in thought, speech and deed. Thirdly he has to meet the bold Ixion whose lust knew no bound, so that he sought to rape even the queen of heaven, Juno, but was caught in a cloud by her, his lustful seed being mutated into the Centaurs, half man, half beast, half reason, half unreason; their progenitor being pinned to the rising and falling wheel of earthly desire that only the purely reasonable man can still with his contempt. Fourthly Orpheus sees the type of covetousness, the ever thirsty, apple-haunted Tantalus, who in life was even willing to please the unknowing gods by giving them his son to eat. He meets Ticius who would have lain with Latona, mother of Apollo god of divination, so that he might have knowledge of events to come, but being over occupied with the many appearances of things, like one half alive (*quasi mortuus*), did not escape the arrows of Apollo and now lies with liver perpetually torn by a vulture. Lastly Orpheus, who should be pure contemplation of the highest good, at first, by the reason in him, seems to win his wife, his desire, towards that upper day, then loses her because the part of him that she represents turns finally to the earth that is really hell. Reason is left to mourn the division from feeling that it had vainly tried to remedy.[14]

Trivet thus narrates the moral psychology of Orpheus in terms that are logical and more dryly abstract than my version would indicate. He does not hint at the hardness of the Boethian way, as does Guillaume. For the latter, significantly, Orpheus is poet as well as wise man, and as the former he betrays reason 'by recalling pleasure or sorrow to the memory rather than guiding and consoling'; at the same time he desires what is good, that desire (somewhat confusingly, and reminiscent of Goethe's principle, *das Ewig Weibliche*, 'the eternal feminine') being represented by his love of Eurydice. Unluckily it is the way of nature to prefer earthly delights and so find hell and grief. Guillaume may harshly conclude of Orpheus the man that 'the dog returns to his vomit', but he does see the poet in the man and the difficulties that the one makes for the other.[15] The concern of the Carthusian interpreter, as might be expected, is more particularly to emphasise the aim of Orpheus, as in his search of the heavens, which represents *contemplatio fervidusque amor summi boni*, the desired experience being a certain *contemplatio . . . quieta*, phrases that are thus rendered by Henryson (448–50), 'the lyf contemplatif,/The parfyt will and als the fervent luf/We suld have allway to the hevin abuf'. Similarly the state of mind that virtuous desire should know, and good poetry inspire, seems to owe something of its description (517–18) to the same source, 'our complexioun/Waxis quyet in contemplacioun'.[16]

In respect of the tale's more important meaning Boccaccio's *Genealogie Deorum* does no more than underscore the traditional interpretation, but it adds significant features to Henryson's narrative. Thus the queen of hell is given her name, Proserpina—a detail sufficient to make the poet turn, as he does, for some slight narrative touches to the popular romance of Sir Orfeo—and Orpheus weeping for his lost wife is said to have resigned himself to live *celebem vitam*, the single life, hence the description 'A woful wedowe' (414), though the latter conveys a human loss not suggested by the anti-feminist Italian. It is in his reference to the Muses, however, that Boccaccio is sub-

stantially influential, and not only for the phrases that
denote their several functions. They gave music, which is
defined as the craft of *moderatio*, the self-control or reason
said to have first attracted Eurydice and finally almost to
have recovered her from hell. It will be remembered that
Henryson's heroine seeks Orpheus, but in Trivet's
account it is Orpheus who seeks her. Following
Macrobius, another source of the Scots poet, Boccaccio
equates the music of the Muses with that of the spheres, a
fancy that, in view of the moral meaning given to the
music, would naturally suggest to Henryson the ironically
conceived search by Orpheus among the planets for the
desire that, as Eurydice, has tragically turned earthwards
and hellwards.[17]

Dante, who sees the musical Orpheus as sage and
healer, would have understood this moral mode of
thinking, but it was alien to Henryson's contemporary,
the Humanist Angelo Poliziano. His *Favola di Orfeo* is
played on a lyre whose harpist seems to listen only to the
always pleasant sounds, whether happy or sad, that he
can bring from it, an exercise in melodious rhetoric. I
cannot accept a recent suggestion that the Scot knew this
recitativo. He had certainly nothing to learn from it. From
the popular romance, in its Scots or English form, he
could at least derive those slight touches of fairy-tale, the
rape of Eurydice by a mysterious Proserpine, her
disappearance into the underworld of 'the fary', that is
also hell, and has a grimly sardonic king Pluto, above all
the encouragement to tell a sustained and movingly
human story with a realised context, and not merely to set
up a frame of moral symbols.

Henryson begins his *Tale of Orpheus And Erudices His
Quene* by affirming and illustrating Aristotle's idea of
'gentill generacioun' as expounded in his *Rhetoric*: noble
spirits breed, or should breed, noble spirit by example and
fame.[18] Thus Orpheus, by the Aristotelian logic, if he falls
away from his inheritance should be marvelled at and con-

demned. Was he not the son of divine Phoebus and the
Muse Calliope, daughter of Jupiter and Memoria?
Calliope being the 'fyndar of all ermonye' and Phoebus, as
Henryson asserts in *The Testament of Cresseid* (200–1), the
causer of 'lyfe in all eirdlie thing', it was natural that their
son Orpheus should be both wonderfully fair to look at
and 'of all musike perfyte', and natural that only for the
fame of his virtues the great queen of Thrace, Eurydice,
should seek him as her husband. In her land, as she
confirms at once on meeting him, he is to be 'king and
lord'.

Surprise that the woman should make the proposal of
marriage has made some readers consider this a feature of
romantic fantasy; alternatively it has evoked different
kinds of moral comment, that by nature Eurydice is
excessively lustful, that she violates the 'hard-to-get'
procedure of courtly love as followed, for example, by
Chaucer's Criseyde. Henryson shows himself aware of
these possible criticisms when he says 'scho thocht no
schame', but the offer is one of marriage and it is within
that sacrament that she gives the 'province' that is her
body as well as Thrace. In *The Kingis Quair* James I of
Scotland had made the doctrinal point clear when he
made the goddess of wisdom declare to the royal lover,

> "Desire", quod sche, "I nyl it noght deny,
> So thou it ground and set in cristin wise".

The Orpheus setting is pagan but the reader understands
that the rules by which its world lives are Christian, and
within marriage the body has its natural rights, so that no
objection is made to there being 'gret play', that is, great
love-making, 'Fra thai war weddit'. It is only sad that the
enjoyment of love should end,

> Lyke till a floure that plesandlie will spring,
> Quhilk fadis sone and endis with murnyng!

The necessary point to make is that Henryson expects

the clerkly reader to recognise the moral meaning in the tragedy that will follow, to reconsider the story once he has read the concluding *Moralitas* and still feel it as a tale of human beings and not merely abstractions. The difficulty of this method is nowhere more obvious than in the following stanzas that narrate Eurydice's death, however visually effective they are. Just as in *The Kingis Quair*, the heroine lightly clad goes out in a May morning 'To tak the dewe and se the flouris spring', modestly accompanied by her 'madin'. Seemingly less lucky than James's 'yong floure', she is desirously seen by a rough keeper of beasts, and the events known to us happen, death comes to the 'medowe grene'. Doubtless Henryson expected a fair degree of understanding in even the first-time reader, that he would know the meadow for the world, the serpent's bite telling him at what level of significance he should be reading, but despite the common reference to the passions as beasts to be kept in order, he could not have expected him at once to identify Aristaeus as virtue making demands that the innocently happy Eurydice was not yet fully ready to meet. Not even the increasing tendency of Scottish religious verse towards the metaphysical conceit, especially in writing about the Christian Calliope, Mary, would have helped. A Scots comparison of her to a pirate on love's seas has been cited, but the application there is clear, as it is in *The Annunciation*, its wonderful first line, 'Forcy as deith is likand lufe', and lines 30–48. Only someone with Henryson's own reading would have understood fully and immediately.

Even so, the rapid sequence of events is effective on its own apparently factual level, making its simple human point that the height of earthly happiness 'fadis sone and endis with murnyng'. That no blame overtly attaches to Eurydice heightens the pathos. The commentaries, Henryson's included, may see her as desire preferring the senses to divine reason or contemplation, and so incurring spiritual death, but in the narrative the poet sees her, as does her husband, dying 'withoutin gilt begild'. What is objectionable in a purely allegorical reading—though this is required at points—is that it debases both hero and heroine, reducing a tragedy to a tale of degeneration. That there is final spiritual loss is true, but in the story-telling that is indeed a final event and not a consequence of this first loss of Eurydice.

Orpheus's angry and grieving response, as already said, amounts to a charge of injustice brought against the gods. He does try to accept their will—'Him to rejos yit playit he a spring'—but in vain. Again, as said, his abandonment of royal state for the wilderness and a dress of 'russet gray' is not the assumption of the palmer's weed but the gesture of rebellious grief, a symbolic rejection of what life has to offer. Orpheus, as the 'barne and childe' protesting the indifference of his divine father to the cross on which the son finds himself, is indeed a voice of puzzled human grief as it has been heard in all ages.

In his bitter complaint he shows the unreasonable state of mind that Boethius was concerned to argue away, and his subsequent pleading search through all the planets is an ironical extension of the same unreason. At the simplest level of appeal what makes this quest so moving is not only its fruitlessness, considering where it is made, but its extreme illustration of the very human desire to escape and deny a painful reality. Orpheus cannot accept that his love is dead, lost to him: so basic a response, the most meaningful aspect of the ancient tale of the resurrection that failed, yet Boethius and his allegorizing commentators do not consider it, and it has had to wait for Henryson's planetary fantasy to language it clearly.

In this case, however, the unreason has a further basic and irremediable aspect, a spiritual one since after all the story must also be read on that level. It is hinted at in the one helpful, knowing if cryptic, direction that the seeker gets among the spheres; Venus, goddess of love, tells her

"trew knicht", "ye mon [must] seike nethir-mare". Love
between man and woman, 'weddit' or not, is naturally of
the flesh, earthly, and the 'hevinlie melody' of which
Orpheus learns something, corresponding to the perfect
reason apprehended by Plato in the heavens, and
accepted by both pagans and Christians as the ideal condition of mind, is not for man, in love or out of it. 'Bot
seldyn thare our appetit is fund,/It is so fast into the body
bund', is Henryson's wholly conventional and wholly
acceptable conclusion in the *Moralitas* 451–2, about the
greatest obstacle to man's pursuit of perfection, man
himself.

En passant one may note characteristic touches of the
poet's down-to-earth humour as evoked by the Platonic
fancy, so alien to his view of life. Orpheus went 'To Mars
the god of batall and of stryf/And socht his speir
[sphere]—yet gat he nocht his wyf'. The poet's comment
on the mystical art of music as described by Boethius and
Macrobius is a shake of the head, 'Of sik musik to wryte I
do bot dote/For in my lyf I couth neuir syng a note', yet
there may be a wry regret for his failure to achieve the
larger music that is his subject.

Of Orpheus on earth it is said, 'ay he fand stretis and
redy wayis' that would take him to the gate of hell. It is
now that his music, which in Master John Ireland's
phrase is 'the regiment of resoun', most stands him in
good stead. The three heads of Cerberus, mortal sin in the
three ages of man, have no power against him; Cerberus
sleeps. The three Furies of ire in thought, word and deed,
let the wheel on which the covetous and lecherous Ixion
turns be stilled, so that their victim escapes. Then
Orpheus has 'rewth' on the ever desirous Tantalus, who is
thus allowed peace. Across the moor of thorns—a Scottish
more than a Greek conception—the harp still has its
saving effect and protects the traveller. Ticius rests from
his vulture (of overmuch curiosity about this world's
affairs). It steadies him on the 'sliddery' way to Pluto and

Proserpine holding court over the endless ranks of the
covetous, kirkmen and laymen.

The harp of reason—the *Moralitas* will say that reason
'wepis wounder saire' for man's failures—has seen
Orpheus safely past the embodied sins that might have
been his, and the sinners' release from pain has shown
what the way of reason could have done for them. Yet the
saving pity is felt to come more from Orpheus, that is
Henryson, than from the doctrine that he upholds and
illustrates, and this is terribly conveyed in his response to
the sight of the hell that he has now reached. These flames
torment, there is no purpose of purification here, no pity.
It is a place of utter hopelessness, not a beginning for a
Divine Comedy, only a scene that accords with the last
words Dante saw over hell's door, 'Lasciate ogni
speranza, voi ch' entrate', 'You who come in, have done
with hope!'.

> O dolly place, and groundless depe dungeoun,
> Furnes of fyre with stynk intollerable,
> Pit of dispaire without remissioun!
> Thy meit vennome, thy drink is poysonable,
> Thy gret panis to compt innomerable;
> Quhat creatur cummis to duell in the
> Is aye deand and never-more may de.

This is a *cri de coeur*, and the horrific sight that prompts it
has no orthodox or logical place in the system of divine
harmony that the poem had posited; on the contrary it
confronts and denies it, even more than Orpheus's first
despairing reaction to the loss of his wife.

At last he sees before him the gray and withered
Eurydice, who returns so brief an answer to her lover's
question about her lost beauty, "ye sall wit the caus ane
othir day". Pluto can jest, "Scho fure [fared] als wele daly
as dois my self". Henryson's awareness of the effectiveness
of a wordless response is almost as evident here as in
Calchas's silent scrutiny of his leprosy-stricken daughter:

Than Orpheus befor Pluto sat doune
And in his handis quhyte his harp can ta.

The music, eliciting a conditional 'remissioun', seems at first to have the same effect as before. From the *Moralitas* we learn why his grim listeners wept; they glimpsed what it could mean, 'Quhen our desyre with resoun makis pes/And sekis up to contemplacioun,/Of syn detestand the abusioun'; that is, with Orpheus all glimpse the rarely realizable, and pity the human condition. What indeed comes across to the concerned reader is the 'reuth and gret pete' that the hero had vainly asked from the higher gods, had put into the cry "Quhar art thow gane my luf Erudices?", and into his horror at the sight of the 'aye deand and never-more may de'. Again, the *Moralitas* may tell us that it is reason widowed of the virtuous 'appetite', as represented by Eurydice, that we are to contemplate when it is said of the self-defeated Orpheus that 'A wofull wedowe hamwart is he went'; but the force of the poet's feeling lies in the phrase 'Bot for a luke', and it is a fact of feeling rather than a moral or ideal that is the story's final meaning for him, "Quhar luf gois, on fors tornes the e".

This may amount to saying that the poem is not a logical work of art; nor is it; the argument of Boethius, the moralizing of Master Nicholas Trivet and his kind, are accepted by the poet but they do not express him. He sees and feels the beauty of the perfection that is inarticulate in their analysis, but he also knows that only a miracle of grace can allow man to achieve it, and he does not expect the miracle to happen, whatever the aspiration and effort. He does expect failure and, regardless of desert, suffering. It has been himself and his tragic viewpoint that he expressed in the lines—

Than perfyte resoun wepis wounder saire,
Seand our appetit thusgate misfaire.

The Tale of Orpheus And Erudices His Quene has faults of

expression or rather want of expression. Things happen or are said in it that the moral postscript has to explain, and does not explain fully, or explains in a fashion that does not truly present the poet's response. That it is defective expression of what the poet has to say is most readily revealed by a comparison with *The Preiching of the Swallow* and *The Testament of Cresseid*. Yet one can regret that romantic elements inherent in the Orphaic story will not reappear in his writing, and recognise that for all its faults this is the most meaningful version of the Orpheus tale in European literature. Its interest can even make us accept a reading procedure that delays understanding and expects a reconsideration. Certainly it is the work of a mind that knows the dimension of vision and questioning into which great poetry should move, and is indeed at some few moments great poetry. At such moments situation and meaning find the words and verse movement to make the simple and profoundly human effect that the myth requires. There are many styles but the simplest says most:

> In his passage amang the planetis all
> He herd ane hevinlie melody and sound
> Passing all instrumentis musicall . . .
> Bot I will tell how Orpheus tuke the way
> To seike his wyf attour the grevis gray
> Hungry and cald, our mony wilsome
>   wane [strange land]
> Withoutin gyde, he and his harpe allane.

NOTES

1. Klaus Heitmann, 'Orpheus im Mittelalter', *archiv fur Kulturgeschichte*, no. 5, 1963, gives the best account of the origin and treatment of the medieval Orpheus.
2. On Guillaume and Denys see Winthrop Wetherbee, *Platonism and Poetry in the Twelfth Century*, 1972, pp. 93–109; Klaus Heitmann, *op. cit.* pp. 276–83. Trivet's account is in *The Poems of Robert Henryson*, ed. G. G. Smith (S.T.S.), I, 1914, pp. liii–lv.

3. M. Nisard, *Macrobe Oeuvres Completes*, Paris, 1863, describes the world's soul in terms of the numbers odd and even (I, p. 20) mentioned by Henryson 225, 338.

4. For Henryson's musical terms see above IV, p. 74, and notes in Elliott's edition. See also Boethius, *De Institutione Musica Libri Quinque*.

5. Boethius, *op. cit.*, I, cap. II.

6. Klaus Heitmann, *op. cit.*, p. 283.

7. Ranald Nicholson, *op. cit.*, pp. 561–62.

8. *St Mark*, 15. v. 34.

9. See my editions of these poems: *Quair*, sts. 26–8; *Hary's Wallace*, II. 180–88.

10. In the Scottish *Saints' Legends*, Scottish Text Society.

11. I. cap. xxxv, referring to Aristotle's *poetria*, the usual term for a 'Poetics'.

12. Vol. 1 (S.T.S.), pp. 40, 164.

13. 'Neoplatonism and Orphism in Fifteenth-Century Scotland', *Scottish Studies*, vol. 20, 1976, p. 74. I do not understand MacQueen; he sees Orpheus as degenerate in seeking Eurydice, regenerate in seeking her in the spheres, losing his regeneration only at the brink of hell; Thrace as the 'unitary soul', hell alone as 'the place of sensual experience'.

14. See note 2 for Trivet.

15. Wetherbee, *op. cit.*, pp. 93–8.

16. Heitmann, *op. cit.*, p. 283.

17. *Genealogie Deorum Gentilium Libri*, ed. Vincenzo Romano, 1951 (Scrittori D'Italia, No. 200), capp. V. 12, VIII. 2.

18. See I. v. 5, ix. 31, 33.

CHAPTER IV

THE MORALL FABILLIS

The Prologue of this collection states the function, method and manner, of its poetry in traditional but exceptionally comprehensive and precise terms. There is the reproof of 'misleving', the conveyance of this 'frute under ane fenyeit fable', the pleasure to be derived from several sources: the interpretation of a 'subtill dyte'—'slee poetry', says Gavin Douglas is not to be understood and appreciated in one easy reading—the estimate of the elicited meaning as being 'to mannis sustenance' or, as Matthew Arnold would have said, 'something on which we can rest', lastly the forms of 'sweit rhetore'. But in his statement of Poetics one line is specially important, 'Amangis ernist to mix ane merie sport', that is, the *Fabillis* is a serious work that intermittently uses comic effects to make its point. Also, it is made clear, its reference is both general and particular. Generally, the actual behaviour of men—who tend to be 'beistis in conditioun', that condition being maintained and even enforced by 'custom and daylie ryte'—is set off against the remote ideal of divine reason. Particularly the poet has in mind Scottish practices and persons. The latter will sometimes be recognised but, in accordance with classical precept, will not be named. It is not for this reason, however, that 'it nedith not record' the name of the lord who proposed the undertaking to Henryson; as has been suggested earlier, this was probably the Lord Abbot, Henry Crichton, who died in 1482. Prologues or prefaces tend to be written last.

Each one of the more important *dicta* here might be found somewhere in writers like St Augustine or Hugh of

St Victor,[1] or the more modern Boccaccio who rated the Aesopic fable among the four great kinds of poem.[2] It is none the less remarkable that one would have to range widely to find mention of all the literary points mentioned above, and that nowhere would they be articulated in such short space, a peculiarly Henrysonian talent. Also very Henrysonian is the pessimistic view that society, and not only human nature, makes it almost inevitable that men should be the 'irrationall' creatures they are. Above all it is characteristic of the poet to see tragedy in this human condition. The author of the *Fabillis* is very much the author of the *Orpheus* and the *Testament*.

It does no harm to recall to the reader, who may associate this *genre* with Chaucer's delightfully light-hearted 'Chanticlere' or with the witty fables of La Fontaine, that Henryson, however individually, works in the main Aesopic tradition of Christian Europe, which offers something other than a sophisticated entertainment for the worldly wise. The difference will be immediately apparent in the very un-Chaucerian character of 'The Taill of the Cok and the Jasp', which begins the series of narratives, as it does in both the *Aesopus* of Gualterus Anglicus and the French Isopets.

Though the *Fabillis* is a collection of tales and not an organically developed work, the desire to 'overgo' previous collections is plain. The number of sources consulted or recalled in the process of creation, for either narration or commentary, shows how deliberate was his work and how much of his serious mind was given to it.

Reading that he certainly exploited for the purely story-telling aspects includes the above-mentioned *Aesopus* (better known as the *Romulus* version, supplemented by the more comprehensive *Monachii Romuleae Et Extravagantes*), the *Fabulae* of Odo of Cheriton, the Latin bestiaries. In French he turned to the popular *Roman du Renart* of Pierre Saint Cloude (in a form close to that edited by Méon), the fourteenth-century *Roman du Renart le*

Contrefait, one of the Isopets not too far from the Lyons text, very probably the free translation made by Julien Macho 1481 of Stainhöwel's Latin collection of 1477, and the tales known as *Le Castoiement D'Un Pere A Son Fils*. It is not certain that he read Caxton's *History of Reynarde the Foxe* 1481 but almost certainly he knew the *Aesop* 1484.

In commentary, among the classics only Aristotle's *Metaphysics* is cited, but the *Ethics* is detectable, and at every point the reader is aware that it is a well-read man who speaks to him. Of course, acquaintance with civil and canon law directs the writer's criticism in several places, it is a one-time student of formal Logic who amuses himself with the notion that beasts no less than men can "Ane sillogisme propone and eik conclude' (46); the Bible and its commentaries suggest or shadow his interpretations, an incident recalls a quotation in a Scots chronicle, and always his pen follows and transmutes the literary fashions of France and England. In brief, identifiable in its sources or not, Henryson's treatment of his fables shows a range of reading, and intellectual awareness of the tendency of his matter, beyond that of any other presentation of the Aesopic world.

There is no profit in trying to review the whole of that presentation under successive aspects. The poems as they present themselves in the accepted text best introduce, and re-introduce, this profound and very various interpreter of life.

The opening tale begins with the few direct strokes that characterise Henryson's brush: a cock merry 'bot pure', 'To get his dennar, set was al his cure', finds a jewel probably swept out of doors by some careless servant-girl. It is 'jolie', very pretty, but nothing to his purpose, "Thow ganis [suits] not for me, nor I for the". It is, of course, the lost treasure of heavenly knowledge, 'tynt and hid', so little sought for that 'Of this mater to speik it wer bot wind', and accordingly the poet dismisses his audience with almost bitter abruptness,

Thairfore I ceis and will na forther say.
Ga seik the jasp quha will, for thair it lay.

As always in Henryson's moralizing there is ambiguity
that proceeds less from what is said than the way, and
spirit, in which it is said. The Isopet, for example, that
the poet has in mind, does not say that the 'jaspe' has been
lost and that it is vain to ask men to seek it, yet the Scot like
the Frenchman does ask after his fashion. He differs
strikingly in the cock's full appreciation of what it rejects,
its sense of the pity of such a choice having to be made, so it
believes, and the world preferred by which it must seek its
'lyfis fud'. Henryson, as the Prologue had already shown
by its reference not only to the bestial inheritance but also
to the influence of 'custum and daylie ryte' in society and
the individual, understands though ideally he cannot
approve the choice. This understanding of the human
dilemma operates everywhere in his fables. Weakness and
its need always have the poet's sympathy, perhaps more
than he sometimes intends, and one may suggest that
what he specially resents in illustrated cases of the wrongs
done by the powerful is their needlessness.

If the situation that Henryson imagines in 'The Taill of
the Cok and the Jasp' is tragic, or tragic in its implications
for the real subject man, that in the story of 'the Upon-
landis Mous and the Burges Mous' is comic; and whatever
moral or religious significances it may carry its lesson is
mainly prudential, a level of treatment that may go far to
explain why the fable has commonly been preferred to
much greater work in the same collection. The emphasis
of treatment is traditional, just as in Walter and *Renart le
Contrefait*,[3] and as it will be in Sir Thomas Wyatt's poem.
MacQueen correctly notices religious overtones, an echo
of St Paul's address to men who make their belly their god,
the Christian meaning of the ominous line, 'The cat
cummis and to the mous hes ee'. But his discovery of
gracelessness in the mice as 'pykaris', petty thieves, and

omitters of grace before meals, finds sinners where there are only mice; his suggestion that the 'spenser' (steward) who unknowingly frightens the 'pykaris' and 'as God wald . . . had na laser for to byde' is God himself perplexes, as also does his notion that 'our jolie cat', who 'throw fortune and gude hap' lets the country mouse scurry beyond his reach, is Fortune herself. Patently the moral of the tale is simply that a life spent 'In quyet and eis' is happiest and best avoids, complete avoidance being impossible, the cat-like spring of Fortune; people that prosper must expect the narrowest escapes.

That Henryson is convinced by his Horatian counsel I am not sure, and concerning the future life of the country mouse one might consider the line, 'I can not tell how weill thairefter scho fure'; but I am certain that he found both sisters amusing, the 'career woman', in modern phrase, who gave herself airs and lived dangerously, and the countrywoman who would never forget her day in town:

> "Wer I into the kith [district] that I come fra
> For weill nor wo suld I never cum agane".

Perhaps like all comic creators Henryson had something of the cat in him and like Walt Disney enjoyed the antics of his unlucky creations; at all events the most vivid moment in his tale is the cat's fun with the briefly captured mouse:

> Fra fute to fute he kest hir to and fra,
> Quhylis up, quhylis down, as cant [playful]
> as ony kid;
> Quhylis wald he lat hir rin under the stra,
> Quhylis wald he wink and play with hir
> buk-heid [game of hide and seek].

The town-mouse has met the cat before, and will doubtless meet him once too often, and the country mouse's escape is only escapism, yet 'escapism' here is felt to be a basic aspect of living. The slightest defences against a cold and always potentially cruel reality are precious. Thus the country sister's 'den' is 'Als warme as woll, suppose it wes not greit'; and the reader responds to this appreciation in the so-called *Moralitas*,

> Thy awin fyre, my freind, sa it be bot a
>   gleid [glowing ember],
> It warmis weill and is worth gold to the.

With the three following tales Henryson's enjoyment of a world that he must none the less deplore becomes explicit. Though 'brutall beistis be irrationall' yet how wonderfully diverse in character and faculties,

> Sa different they ar in properties,
> Unknawin to man, and sa infinite,
> In kynd havand sa fell [many] diversities.

Amusement and criticism go together.

The bestial (human) comedy, so long as it is viewed as such, for proper illustration needs its clever clown, its witty fool, alternately victor and victim in the predatory game, and tradition has elected the fox 'craftie and cawtelous' [full of wiles]. Here various sources helped, along with the versions of Aesop the *Roman de Renart* and *Roman du Renart le Contrefait*. His was the way of the world; his victories exposed weakness, his defeats asserted the sureness of Nemesis, the certainty of Fortune's changes, the inevitability of death. Of course, being humanity itself, he has the author's and our sympathies. Notably Henryson suggests no equation with the devil such as we find in the bestiaries and even implied in Chaucer's description.

It is a little surprising that he should be introduced with a tale that Chaucer had already told so brilliantly, that of his foiled attempt on the life of Chanticlere. The choice invited comparison. Perhaps the temptation to underscore the Englishman's mock-heroic effects was irresistible, hence the echo of romance in the widow's out-cry,

"Allace, now lost is gentill Chanticleir!", and in her addressing the dogs as if they were knights of the household,

> "Reskew my nobill cok or he be slane,
> Or elles to me se ye cum never agane!"

But though similar opportunities are taken with the reactions of the cock's three hens—"Quha sall our lemman be? Quha sall us leid?", etc.—the motive for introducing these new characters, perhaps the excuse for the whole new version, is more likely to have been the desire to balance the hypocrisy of the enemy with the same unexpected quality at home. As Hary in his epic poem, apparently remembered in the comic laments, had observed, no traitor like the 'weile trastyt in-born familiar'.[4]

The hen Pertok has no sooner done with the due, if premature, lamentations for the communal husband than her sister Sprutok is prepared to sing "Wes never wedow so gay!", the recovered Pertok to expect the attentions of a more satisfactory lover, and Toppok, 'lyke ane curate crous' [bold], to see in the supposed death "the verray hand of God" punishing for "kittokis [mistresses] ma than sevin". Chaucer's courtly Pertelote, depressingly practical as she may be, gives no sign of belonging with this suddenly unfaithful company.

The contrast presented by the poems is remarkable. Chaucer's is a literary delight to be read on the same level as Alexander Pope's *Rape of the Lock*. It is a learned entertainment, and is not substantially Aesopic in the sense of having a serious human reference and making a serious moral point. This is Henryson's contribution. Even his more plainly farcical treatment helps here. Not only is the theme of hypocrisy sharpened by its extension to those who do not have the fox's need to 'loif [praise] and le', and by the rapid shift from grieving eulogy to wildly scandalous criticism, but an odd turn of sympathy for the 'revar' is developed, so appreciatively eager does he appear in the anticipation of his prey,

> "Quhen I behald your fedderis fair and gent,
> Your beik, your breist, your hekill and your kame,
> Schir, be my saull and the Blissit Sacrament,
> My hart is warme, me think I am at hame.
> To mak yow blyth I wald creip on my wame
> In froist and snaw, in wedder wan and weit,
> And lay my lyart [gray] lokkis under your feit."

He may be "ane verray vengeance from the hevin", but it is the cock who gets that description, and when the latter cleverly escapes it is the disconsolate fox, left to feel foolish, who is most remembered. This balance of representation is maintained in the altogether serious *Moralitas*; here again, one notes, it is the cock in his pride who suggests the allusion to the devil. A typical Henrysonian hit, perhaps prompted by Chaucer's *seigneurial* picture of Chanticlere, is aimed at lords emptily proud of 'kin and blude'.

One waits for the further adventures of Reynard, or Lowrence (that is, the lurker) as Henryson prefers to call him. From the reading of *Renart le Contrefait*, 23569–23601, comes the picture in the sequent tale of the 'Confessioun' of the fox on a high hill reading into the stars his mortal destiny, and panicked by the sense of sin. Blessings on his father who gave him a good university education (648)! And luckily here comes that 'worthie Doctour in Divinite/Freir Wolf Waitskaith'. Absolution from so holy a source, as a Gray Friar is bound to be, must make up for whatever is still missing in the penitent.

There are mentions of such a confession in several narrative sources, and the sins confessed in some are more startling but Henryson's is much the more dramatic rendering, and he gains relevant effect by sticking to the sins that the reiving fox-nature can never give up. About this

Lowrence is quite frank, he cannot repent being his
unalterable self,

> Me think that hennis ar sa honie-sweit,
> And lambes flesche that new ar lettin bluid;
> For to repent my mynd can not concluid
> Bot of this thing—that I haif slane sa few.

And, of course, having the instincts of a gentleman, he can
only take; he cannot be expected to beg, much less work.
By way of punishment he will restrict himself to black
puddings since they have a little blood in them, and the
extremities or less solid parts of the creatures he kills.
Naturally he gets his absolution, for the Gray Friar from
his own experience well understands that 'neid may haif
na law'.

It is the same need that allows the penitent to perform
the subsequent miracle. The Firth of Forth—for the wild
waves at 736 can only belong to the firth near Dunfermline
abbey—does not encourage fishing that day, but a flock of
goats appears, and so, "Ga doun Schir Kid, cum up Schir
Salmond agane!" A clever confusion of the rites of
baptism, conferment of knighthood, and the transubstan-
tion of the mass, has produced one good meal. And the sun
is shining. The happy hypocrite, stroking his full belly in
the pleasant warmth, reflects that if death's arrow is to
strike, now is the time. It does, since the keeper of the goats
has spotted him. Protesting at a too literal-minded destiny
the fox exclaims,

> "Me think na man may speik ane word in play
> Bot nowondayis in ernist it is tane."

(There may be a reader who remembers the Viking in the
saga who, in spite of a crushed skull, found time to remark,
'These new-fangled axes are all the rage').

This piece of fantastic wit is perhaps the most amusing
of Henryson's tales, and on a serious consideration, for its
stressed conflict between what is right and what seems, or

actually is, necessary, one of the most disturbing. The *Moralitas* may end with the insistent requirement, 'Obey unto your God', but the greater part of its commentary, like the illustration in the tale, has stressed the practical impossibility of such obedience. It stresses the sweetness that man's nature finds in sin, the needs that his nature imposes on him. The daily demands of society seem to be implied in the legal concept of 'consuetude and ryte' (782)—'consuetude' is a recurring phrase in Henryson— alongside the ordinary sense of the continuing force of habit. When he writes (786–89),

> Use drawis nature swa in propertie
> Of beist and man, that neidlingis thay
>   maun [must] do
> As thay of lang tyme hes bene hantit to,

one remembers lines from Wordsworth's *Intimations of Immortality*,

> And custom lie upon thee with a weight
> Heavy as frost, and deep almost as life.

(One may even think of politicians who use a pre-nuclear rhetoric to justify a nuclear war). In Henryson unlike Wordsworth, it is indeed the expected course of things that the 'vision splendid' should 'die and fade away/Into the light of common day'. It may be objected that so heavy a text spoils a light story but not for the intelligent reader.

Much less effective is 'The Taill of the Sone and Air of the foirsaid Foxe callit Father Wer' [worse than the father], which has earlier been conveniently mentioned as the tale of the 'Parliament'. It is, as it were, a collocation of scenes that do not amount to a play, and has a peculiarly detached epilogue. The author specifies his theme, the worldling's guilty conscience that sees 'suddand deith draw neir with panis sore' (1137), but he does not visualise it with conviction, or find a consistent and natural alterna-

tion between the comic and serious modes of thought. He
has had a variety of ideas, from various sources, that
supplied pictures but did not support the overall topic.
Both the French *romans* are remembered in the Parliament of Beasts, though it is developed in the procedural
terms of a Scottish parliament; Holland's *Buik of the
Howlat* helps the description of the lion's crown; *The Kingis
Quair*, quoted, supplies the precedent for a listed proces-
sion of animals, while Bower's *Scotichronicon* actually
provides a facetiously applied Latin line; and the
embassies to Renart that the romances mention are
replaced by recourse to Odo of Cheriton's fable of the wolf
and fox discomfited by an ass, here a mare, whose
privilegium ('privilage' 1058), exemption from parlia-
mentary attendance, was the force of its hoof, though the
romances know this episode in another context. An
embarras or confusion of riches.

The tale begins promisingly and originally, this fox
thanking God for the death of his restrictive father but
retaining enough 'natural pietie' to give the body burial in
the nearest bog. But we have scarcely met this good son
when he is startled by the bugle of the Unicorn pursuivant
(suitably, since that is the title of one of the Scots heralds),
proclaiming a parliament that must, his guilty conscience
tells him, expose his many crimes. To villainy like his it
seems that the bugle 'maid all the warld to waig' [shake].
The lion who presides so awefully, and absurdly—he
opens proceedings with an appropriately terrifying leap so
that 'flatlingis to his feit thay fell all doun'—makes a very
Roman claim, *parcere prostratis et debellare superbos*, more
simply, "I rug [rend], I reif [spoil] all beistis that makis
debait". It is a claim that the Scottish Lion could seldom
make, and if the story assures us that this lion rules 'with
richteousnes' the *Moralitas* sees him only as the driving
way of the world. Indeed at this point Henryson has his
tongue firmly in his cheek, as appears in the farcically
played fears of the fox. He tears his hair, arrives in court

with pretended limp and loss of one eye, dodges vainly behind the other beasts to avoid notice, only to find that the lion has no worse use for him than to go with the wolf on a mission to the *contumax* mare, who expresses her opinion of all parliaments and courts by staying away from them.

What follows, the 'reid bonnet' of a Doctor of Divinity conferred on the rashly officious wolf by the mare's hoof, is excellent 'slapstick', heightened by the fox's sudden revelation of a learning that he had prudently denied, "*Felix quem faciunt aliena pericula cautum*", which the lion king duly renders as 'The hurt of ane happie the uther makis'. He is also happy to observe that 'The greitest clerkis ar not the wysest men'. Just as amusing is the confirmation of the fox's first fears when his 'bludie snout', convicts him of the recent murder of a lamb. A speech at the gallows' foot, where he is shriven by the wolf, is, one feels, sadly missing, but it would have added little to the confession of his late unlamented father.

That Henryson's imagination is unwilling to give any serious depth to his comic tale appears in its few moments of mock sermonising, as on the fox's dodging game in court: 'Thy cheir changis Lowrence, thow maun luke doun./Thy worship of [dignity in] this warld is went away'. Similarly one cannot take seriously the fantastic commentary, where it is said of that allegedly ideal Christian, the mare, 'Hir hufe I likkin to the thocht of deid' [death]. Perhaps least of all would the poet expect the reader to recite aloud with all seriousness the last stanza, which opens with prayer, 'O Mediatour mercifull and meik', and closes with a chuckle, 'And thus endis the talking of [about] the tod' [fox]. A very funny tale, with an overall comic view of authority at its business of justice and the subject at his game of evading it, but without the full involvement, and continuity of 'decorum' into the *Moralitas*, that Henryson's best story-telling displays.

If this poem comes near to rivalling the paradoxes of sensibility that one encounters in the alternating license and piety of the poet's contemporary, Luigi Pulci, the same cannot be said of the sequent 'Scheip and the Dog'. Here the involvement is profound and continuous in tale, theme and commentary. Not only this, but there is a consistency of tone, a sustained factualness and bareness of statement, that intensifies feeling and has much more than a prosaic effect. The poetical success has doubtless something to do with his notary's knowledge of consistorial court procedure, much more with the feeling that justice, or rather injustice, always rouses in him, and most with the conveyance of a vision beyond the statement. Readers soon become aware how often the word 'pure' recurs in Henryson, and of the further sense of 'pitiable' that it carries, as in the immediate direction of feeling at the outset of the argument, 'How that ane doig, because that he was pure/Callit ane scheip to the consistorie'.

Full appreciation of the poem naturally requires a recognition of the legal aspect that was so familiar to Henryson, and this has been fully supplied by E. M. W. Rollins.[5] The style at once grave and familiar is readily appreciable in these lines now to be quoted, but one has also to know the concept in Scottish law called by Lord Hailes 'the lawless hour', that is, times in which trials are not permissible:

> The selie scheip durst lay na mouth on eird
> Till he befoir the awfull juge appeird,
> The oure off caus quhilk that the juge usit than
> Quhen Hesperus to schaw his face began.

Injustice is perhaps the most emotive of subjects. If Shakespeare's *Lear* has a defect it is its extreme excitation without quietening of feeling, the uncontrolled passion of its protest. What Henryson works towards is the quiet finality of statement in the last line of description of the sheep's destitution, 'Naikit and bair syne to the feild couth

pas', or an effect as simple as that of the Psalmist's
question, "Lord God, quhy sleipis Thow sa lang?" Abandoned even by the church, 'We pure pepill as now may do
no moir/Bot pray to The', and hope that heaven will give
'gude rest' to our sufferings.

'The Taill of the Lyoun and the Mous' has a political
reference that has been already considered, so plain that
'king and lord may weill wit quhat I mene'. This needs no
further notice here, but the imagined context and what is
characteristic in the more general comment does, because
it has hardly been considered. The poet has a vision and
gives to the June scene a correspondingly ideal beauty,
'The blossumis blythe brak upon bank and bra'. Into the
visioned scene strides Aesop himself, a splendid figure,
vital with authority, no longer the hunchback of tradition
since his dwelling now 'is in hevin for ay':

> His beird was quhyte, his ene wes grit and gray,
> With lokker [curling] hair quhilk over his
>   schulderis lay.

He gives it as his opinion (clearly also Henryson's) that
moral tales are quite ineffectual "Quhen haly preiching
may nathing availl", an observation that Lessing was to
repeat: didactic literature makes no converts, it serves
only to confirm the virtuous in their virtue. That he
indulges the poet with a fable implies no contradiction.
The beauty about him he dismisses in the *Moralitas*,
"Richt as the rois with froist and wynter weit/Fadis, swa
dois the warld". Like the countrymen in his tale who
caught the lion, men do not learn to look beyond their
present harms, "For hurt men wrytis in the marbill
stane". The recent imprisonment of the Scots king by
rebels and Henryson's strong disapproval of their action
do not explain entirely this despondency, not even the
interruption of 'justice' (1618) that inevitably ensued. We

have to look to Henryson's view of what he calls the
'canker' in human nature.

The greatest of the fables, and with *The Testament of
Cresseid* one of Henryson's two greatest poems, is *The
Preiching of the Swallow*. Its argument proceeds from the
perfection and creative goodness of God to the destruction
and damnation of his creatures, and the necessity for
another and compensating world; it proceeds with a
movement of thought and action, beauty and pity, that
conveys inevitability and at the same time a question. The
measured verse, the weighted and feeling choice of scenes
and words, make us aware of a poetic sensibility of the first
order.

Henryson's reading as deployed in this poem goes far
beyond the detectable sources. The several stated distinc-
tions between the natures of God and man, the very
definite distrust of 'ressoun naturall' and indeed of any
argumentation about matters of faith—'trow fermelie and
lat all ressoun be'—show the conservative, and troubled,
theologian. Of course, he knew more of Aristotle than the
Metaphysics which he cites for an effective image, and more
on the harmony of nature than the obviously remembered
De Institutione Musica of Boethius.[6] Among vernacular texts
consulted is certainly an Isopet, his fondness for the
discursive *Renart le Contrefait* is again evident,[7] and touches
come in from *The Kingis Quair* (as noted by MacQueen)
and from Hary's *Wallace*. Naturally he tries to think
within Christian terms, yet the individual direction that
he gives to his matter or argument can lead the reader to a
response that is not specifically Christian at all. The poet,
like his Swallow, considers a universal truth of human
weakness and its consequence. The birds that are the
fowler's victims are fools; that they are so and must suffer
for it is felt to be tragic because they are mankind.

It is not peculiar to Henryson's version of the fable that
the omniscience of God, as it comprehends all times,

should be mentioned. Isopet I asserts it though in the *moralité*. What is peculiar is the stress he puts on its statement, brought here to the very beginning of the poem, still more the slant of meaning that is given to it. *En passant* it should be observed that appreciation depends not only on recognition of what is happening but also, from the first stanza, on catching with the spiritual ear, as it were, the high and simple dignity of tune with which the poet begins his incantation. To facilitate recognition of this aspect accents have been supplied in the lines now quoted.

> The hie prudènce and wirking mervelous,
> The pròfound wit off God omnipotent,
> Is sa perfyte and sa ingenious,
> Excelland far all mannis jugëment:
> Forquhy to Him all thing is ay presènt
> Rycht as it is, or ony tyme sall be,
> Befoir the sicht off His Divinitie.

Man in his dungeon of flesh has no such advantage. Like the bat, in Aristotle's comparison, he is blind in the sunlight of truth and lives in a world of dark 'fantasye', guessing at things that should be 'manifest' to sight and reason. Astronomy should teach us 'That God in all His werkis wittie is'; his diverse creatures, and especially man made in his own form, should show that everywhere God is 'fair and gude'. The structure of our earth where everything is 'Concordand till our opurtunitie' (1676) should tell us the same thing. Consider the seasons, perfect in their succession and individually, thus the autumn:

> Syne harvest hait [hot], quhen Ceres that
>   goddes
> Hir barnis benit [crammed] hes with abundance,
> And Bacchus god of wyne renewit hes
> The tume pyipis [emptied casks] in Italie
>   and France

> With wynis wicht [strong] and liquor off
>   plesance,
> And *Copia Temporis* to fill hir horne,
> That neuir was full off quheit nor uther corne.

and duly springtime,

> The secretar off somer with his sell [seal],
> Quhen columbie [columbine] up-keikis [peeps up]
>   throw the clay
> Quhilk fleit [frightened] wes befoir with
>   froistis fell [cruel].

Seemingly, if one forgot the menace of those first stanzas, a perfect world, and innocent of all but the promise of seedtime to the poet observing ploughmen and sowers: 'It wes grit joy to him that luifit corne'.

But suddenly he hears the Swallow warn that it is not all corn-seed that is being sown; there is also linseed that will grow and be made into nets to catch the birds. The process of flax-making, like the farmer's business, was something that Henryson had often watched around Dunfermline, and he describes it precisely in lines 1825–31. The nature of the nets, physical and spiritual, scarcely needs the comment of the *Moralitas*. What does need comment is the sinister correspondence of the stages of the lint's growth and final, fatal use, through spring, summer and winter, to the succession of the seasons extolled as illustrating God's beneficent order. The nets, concealed with chaff, are laid, but it is winter, the birds must shelter and eat, and less than ever can they listen to the Swallow.

> The wynter come, the wickit wind can blaw,
> The woddis grene wer wallowit [wasted] with
>   the weit,
> Baith firth and fell with froistys wer maid
>   faw [discoloured],
> Slonkis [hollows] and slaik [valley] maid
>   slidderie with the sleit,

The foulis fair for falt [want] thay fell off feit;
On bewis bair it wes na bute [help] to byde,
Bot hyit [hurried] unto houses thame to hyde.

The chaff is taken, the birds netted, and so—

Allace, it wes grit hartsair for to se
That bludie bowcheour beit thay birdis doun!

What the *Moralitas* tells us is that man, being the fool he
is, will follow the way of the world, whose attractiveness,

Lyke to the mow [chaff] befoir the face of wind
Quhiskis away and makis wretchis blind.

Even for its time it is a poetical sermon of singular
hopelessness. What are we to make of the story's last lines,
of the despairing departure of the Swallow, not to be seen
again by the poet?

"This grit perrell I tauld thame mair than
    thryis.
Now ar thay deid and wo is me thairfoir!"
Scho tuke hir flicht bot I hir saw no moir.

The final stanza of the *Moralitas* advises prayer but, as was
also apparent in the tales of 'The Cok and the Jasp' (159)
and 'The Lyoun and the Mous' (1390), there is no
expectation that the advice will be effectual in any
practical respect. The Swallow, likened to 'The halie
preichour' and by extension connoting Christ, may
indeed take its flight. It is not only something like despair
that drives the poet, there is horror, also shown in the
Orpheus, for the orthodox imagining of the destiny of most
men, 'The Saull to fyre, to everlestand pane'; and there is
pity for creatures who could scarcely be expected to do
other than they did.

To convey the human situation in this painful way
Henryson has set God's omniscience against man's
ignorance and sacrifice of everything to a present need, the

utility and beauty of the created world against man's
natural failure to respond worthily to them, the *Copia
Temporis* against the destitution of winter and the hell
outside time. And in case his feelings should go
unrecognised he has given the well known fable an ending
quite different from that in the many other versions. In all
others the Swallow advises once or twice, and then prudently sells its silence to the fowler for shelter in his
thatched roof. Their Swallow is a man of the world, a
realist. But here Swallow and poet are too concerned for
the birds to consider any such compact. There is great art
in the poem that goes beyond the odd felicitous expression
or dramatic effect. Also, to the intention, the construction
and the language, can be applied Wilfred Owen's saying
about his war poems, 'the poetry is in the pity'.

The Wolf that gat the Nek-hering [the pick of the herring] is
an ironic title, since the wolf, trying to imitate the fox's
pretence of death so that he will be thrown beside the
carter's desirable fish, gets only a painful beating. A
section of the *Roman de Renart* has been embroidered upon
to make a tale that the poet tells only for enjoyment of the
fox's fantastic trickery.[8] A vivid phrase or two halts the
reader, as in Renard's mouth-watering praise of the best
herring, "It is a syde of salmond, as it wair,/And callour
[fresh], pypand [weeping] lyke ane pertrik [partridge's]
ee". The *Moralitas* is perfunctory except for the notice of
the power of money to set armies moving, 'Richt swa the
gold garris landis and cieties/With weir be waistit daylie
as men seis'.

In *The Taill of the Foxe that begylit the Wolff in the schadow of
the Mone* it is indeed moonshine that floods the story.
Again we have two fantastic tales united, but this time as
fantastic a *Moralitas*, and the pleasure in each case derives
from a species of fantastic wit.

A ploughman loses his temper with skittish oxen, rashly

'gives' them to the wolf, is overheard by the wolf who has the fox for witness, and forthwith finds himself caught in the more ancient procedures of extra-curial law.[9] The fox, in a famous phrase applied by John Barbour to Edward I of England, agrees to be 'ane juge amycabill', that is, 'compositour' or arbitrator, whereupon 'The wolf braid [thrust] forth his fute, the man his hand,/And on the toddis [fox's] taill sworne thay ar to stand'. Since the case, like that in 'The Scheip and the Doig', is to be decided in 'a lawless hour', bribes are in order, explains the fox, accepting a gift of hens, "For God is gane to sleip; as for this nycht/Sic small thingis ar not sene into His sicht' . The wolf is placated by the promise of a wonderful cheese and at last sees it shining 'pennyful' from a well where, explains Renard, it has been hidden by that cunning ploughman, "Quhyte as ane neip [turnip] and round als as ane seill,/He hang it yonder that na man suld it steill". In the fantasy carried over into the *Moralitas* we learn that the cheese is this shining world, 'that wickit well' is hell, and (an explanation worthy of the fox) 'The hennis ar warkis that fra ferme faith proceidis'.

If in the *Preiching* the poet sees Fortune's world as tragic, here he chooses to see it as wholly absurd, the absurdity being conveyed with a well maintained gravity that has the force of wit. As the wolf's heavy greed carries him down in the bucket to help lift his glittering prize, the fox naturally rises in his so that they briefly meet:

> Than angerlie the wolff upon him cryis,
> "I cummand thus dounwart, quhy thow upwart
>   hyis?"
> "Schir", quod the foxe, "thus fairis it off
>   Fortoune,
> As ane cummis up scho quheillis ane uther doun!"

The substance of the exchange is not original; the Voltairean neatness of its delivery, and the implication that it shares with other dialogue in the poem, is.

'The Taill of the Wolf and the Wedder' is a very spirited rendering of, it would seem, the similar but very drably told tale in Caxton's *Aesop*. The chase of the wolf by the sheep in a dog's skin is given a pace and physical actuality supplied by no other version. Henryson's characteristic humour of fantasy briefly shows in the wolf's amazed gaze at the exposed pursuer, "Richt now a hound, and now quhyte as ane freir!", and the characteristic wit enters with the sheep's ready but weak apology, "Ane flear gettis ane follower commounly". In the first stanza of the *Moralitas* one notes the brief but surprising descent to Lydgatian levels of diction, and elsewhere the warning to 'pure men' not to be 'presumteous' that is equally surprising, since not at all a characteristic theme, until one remembers that contemporary reference (noticed here in an earlier chapter): the rebellion of 1482 and hanging of the king's servants. Despite the descriptive merits and odd Henrysonian touches, it is felt that the poet has put much less of himself than is usual into his story-telling.

It is otherwise with 'The Taill of the Wolff and the Lamb'. Here there is nothing of the spirit and effect that he once advocated, 'Quhen the complexioun waxis quyet in contemplacioun'. It treats of the theme that most moves him, injustice, and may be said to burn with a flame of indignation that steadily increases. In the tale his protest has the control of narrated circumstance, the picked quarrel, the pretence of formal argument, the foreseen conclusion; in the *Moralitas* it has the release of denunciation and prayer. As in his other treatments of this theme, but especially here, story and *Moralitas* are felt as one, in this case the further development in specific charges carrying even more weight than its generalised or symbolised introduction

The simplicity and directness of approach are impressive. In the first stanza and first line of the second the menace of the situation is made clear. The 'selie' [defenceless] lamb comes to the stream, 'Bot of his fa the wolff nathing he wist/And in the streme laipit to cule his thrist . . . Thus drank thay baith—bot not of ane intent'. Though the water flows to where the lamb is, the wolf higher up accuses him of fouling his drink. Both creatures at first act and argue as if there were a justice to be appealed to. The lamb's appeal to laws physical, social, divine, should be amusing and is not; similarly the wolf's shift of ground to a charge against the lamb's murdered father, the language of 'Halie Scripture' that both use, and the accuser's final statement of his real position;

> "Na!", quod the wolff. "Thow wald intruse
>   ressoun
> Quhair wrang and reif suld duell in propertie
>   [by right].
> That is ane poynt and part of fals tressoun
> For to gar reuth remane with crueltie.
> Be His woundis, fals tratour, thow sall de
> For thy trespas, and for thy fatheris als!"
> With that anone he hint [seized] him by the
>   hals [neck].

Within varying limits this, in Henryson's view, is how the world decides its arguments.

The formal argument here has an interest beyond its story occasion, and even its social application, because of the religious import of two opposing statements. The poet gives peculiar weight to one part of the wolf's pretended case, an alleged crime of the lamb's father. The lamb, knowing *Ezekiel* xviii, protests, "Schir, it is wrang that for the fatheris gilt/The saikles [innocent] son suld punist be or spilt"; the wolf, remembering *Exodus* xx, ('for I the Lord thy God am a jealous God, visiting the iniquities of the fathers upon the Children unto the third and fourth generation'), will 'refuse [exempt] nane off his successioun'. The wolf's interpretation is not 'twisted', as MacQueen asserts. There is a real opposition of texts.

Henryson simply prefers one to the other. What is at issue is divine justice as well as human justice. In that period the latter could hardly be considered except in the context of the former, but the intensity of Henryson's concern with the issue is exceptional. He will duly give a contemporary application to the murder of the lamb, but the common use of that harmless creature as an emotive Christian symbol—'he was led as a lamb to the slaughter'—is surely in his mind when he writes the tale's last three lines:

> Of his murther quhat sall we say, allace?
> Wes not this reuth—wes not this grit pietie,
> To gar [cause] this selie lamb but [without]
>   gilt thus de?

Naturally the theme is still given a religious expression in the *Moralitas*, though the lamb is now 'the pure pepill'. The life of workers on the land is 'half ane purgatorie', and the exploiting landlord with his servile lawyer 'cryis ane vengeance unto the hevinnis hie', the justice of hellfire. In the first line of the concluding prayer, 'God keip the lamb, quhilk is the innocent', though it follows a listing of specific wrongs to be righted, the hoped-for justice is less on earth than in heaven.

With a true poet the story he tells develops its own meaning, not entirely the one that he proposes for it. This is very much the case with Henryson's 'Taill of the Paddok [toad] and the Mous'. A memory of the short Latin version provides one of the few amusing moments in Dante's *Inferno*,[10] and the Scottish poet's amusement with his own picturesque development of the fable infects and overcomes his moral commentary. The story begins with a joke, the *Moralitas* becomes jocular,

> Adew my friend! And gif that ony speiris
>   [asks why]
> Of this fabill sa schortlie I conclude,
> Say thow I left the laif [rest] unto the
>   freiris
> To mak exempill and ane similitude.

Even the last line of this final stanza, which prays to Christ
'Grant us til pas intill ane blissit hour', has a dismissive
air: there will be no more fables. Henryson's scepticism
about the practical value of any moral story-telling has
already been remarked on.

The action begins with a heroine in a hurry,

> Ane lytill mous come till ane rever-syde:
> Scho micht not waid, hir schankis [legs]
>   were sa schort;
> Scho culd not swyme, scho had na hors to ryde.

But a toad offers to be ferryman, and argues so reasonably
against her instinctive discrimination against his race and
repulsive appearance that at last she cries, "Lat be thy
preiching!", and being frantic with hunger for the barley
and oats on the farther side agrees to be tied to his leg by a
thread. Of course, he tries to drown her, and just as she is
crying for a priest a watching kite seizes and eats both.

Vainly does Henryson tell us that the mouse is man's
soul, the toad his body, the field of barley and oats
'hevinnis bliss', and the kite death that finds us
unprepared for heaven. Man's mortal life of physical and
spiritual conflict becomes thus as absurd as the terms in
which it is told. What keeps a serious meaning for reader
and poet alike is the tale's conveyance of the irrationality
and menace of this demanding world of Fortune. The toad
has indeed a jewel in its head (2835–36):

> The blaberyis, thocht thay be sad of hew,
> Ar gadderit up quhen primerose is forsakin.

And the articulateness of the poet's sympathy for the
human condition has its value; like struggling toad and
mouse we are all 'swymmand air and lait/Into this warld
with cairis implicate' (2937–38). It is at this level of
struggle with life and death that Henryson touches us. In
the tale as a whole, however, he goes beyond serious
responses; the deadly conflict has become a comedy, a
farce.

The variety of treatments in the *Morall Fabillis* reflects the variety of impressions that life makes on the poet, yet it is recognisably the same experience that is always described, the same tragi-comic vision, the same sense of living in a fantastic world that animates them. It is a world that knows injustice, and Henryson's anger against powerful and ruthless interests is plain. It asks for pity because its fools cannot help being what they are, 'beistis irrationall'. Yet one can make too much of the present needs that make the Cock reject his jewel and the birds pay no heed to the Swallow, for life is not always 'half ane purgatorie'; in respect of its injustices it is not always true that 'as for this nycht/Sic small thingis ar not sene into His sicht'. For the most part the driving needs do find their satisfaction before 'the cat cummis'. There is even beauty if the 'beistis' care to look for it. Certainly it is a world that evokes intense responses. Above all it is an entertainment, and the poet who considers it is as amused as saddened by it. As a philosophic humourist, seeing his own kind in the antics of these creatures he would readily agree that if man did not exist it would be necessary to invent him.

The art of the poet is as various as his creations. It is most impressive when he expresses the extremes of distress or absurdity, when his involvement is continuous in tale and comment, and the rôle of preacher or entertainer is maintained throughout.

NOTES

1. Marie Comeau, *La Rhétorique de Saint Augustin*, Paris, 1930; B. F. Huppé, D. W. Robinson, *Fruyt and Chaf Studies in Chaucer's Allegories*, 1963.
2. *ibid.*, p. 18.
3. vol. 2, pp. 239–41.
4. For the rhetoric see *Wallace*, XII. 1114–24, for the quotation I. 112.
5. 'Robert Henryson and the Scottish Courts of Law', *Aberdeen University Review*, xxxix, 1962, pp. 219–26.

6. *De Institutione Musica Quinque Libri*, I. 2: each season bears its own fruits and helps the others to bear theirs; so, in Henryson, spring like a good secretary brings the seal that its master summer will use (1707).

7. *Renart Le Contrefait*, 23573–601, 33923–38, 35143.

8. *Roman de Renart*, ed. M. D. M. Méon, 3538–4260.

9. Craig MacDonald, 'The Perversion of Law in Robert Henryson's Fable of the Fox, the Wolf, and the Husbandman', is a useful study soon to be published.

10. See close of canto 22, beginning of canto 23.

CHAPTER V

THE TESTAMENT OF CRESSEID

It was the distinct recollection of one guest at the banquet described by Plato that at its close he woke sufficiently from the effect of too much wine, to understand that Socrates was telling the tragic poet Agathon and the comic poet Aristophanes that the ideal poet would perform equally well in both kinds. On a first consideration one feels that the guest must have misheard, but there is the fact of Shakespeare to suggest that the philosopher and not his poetical friends was on the right side of the argument. The bias of time and circumstance has indeed a great deal to do with the way a poet chooses to employ his powers—if he is allowed to choose. Greek convention made for specialism. Shakespeare found himself on a stage that encouraged him to be what his rival Greene called him, 'an absolute *Johannes factotum*'. What circumstances encouraged Henryson, in such little space, to display such variety of excellence, is less easy to state. Beyond the unsettled and exploratory spirit of Scottish culture in his day, which prompted self-expression in many forms, I can only refer to the variety of his practical experience. Though all aspects of that would constantly have their effect, I find myself thinking of the *Orpheus* as specially reflecting the priest and the scholar, the *Fabillis* the schoolmaster and lawyer, and the *Testament* the man who had the care of the hospital at the town's gates.

We do not know—having so unreliable a reporter— whether Socrates touched on the kind of mind that would excel in such seemingly different modes of expression. It would have been unlike him to be so subjective, yet it can be suggested. Of course, sympathetic acceptance of 'men as they come', to a measured point, would be one quality; it would have to be, as it was in Henryson's case, a mind that was always intense, basically serious and critical, yet open and various in its responses, above all, apprehending the aspect of fantasy in the business of life and death and ready to give itself equally to the extremes of that fantasy. This readiness has been witnessed in the very differing effects of individual fables, even if the Aesopic terms of treatment naturally seem to give them an overall comic bias, and now it is witnessed in the unqualified magnification of the sufferings of one significant person.

Though the cosmic context that is necessary to give full religious and philosophic magnitude to such an action is present in the *Orpheus*, always appealed to in the Fables, where the *Preiching* is its greatest statement, it is the *Testament* that makes most effective use of it. Here indeed Henryson, exploiting concepts from the pseudo-science of astrology that he did not himself approve of, gives his story a visualised supra-human dimension, realised with an intensity that European literature had only known before in Dante and the Greeks, a reference that was only permitted to appear momentarily and suggestively in the secular tragedy of Shakespeare. The comparative advantages of such a context are apparent in the closing scene of Marlowe's *Faustus*, even in Goethe's poem where Mephistopheles is only a more impressive than usual eighteenth-century *philosophe*, and, among many modern works that have similarly tried to give their subject a further dimension, *Peer Gynt*.

The *Testament* can be responded to and admired *per se*, but additional to the general reference there is a particular and specifically literary one. Just as one cannot properly recognise and evaluate the original achievement that the *Troilus and Criseyde* of Chaucer represents, without knowing that side of the English poet's work appreciated

by a French contemporary in the phrase, 'ce grant translateur', his very extensive rendering of Boccaccio's *Il
Filostrato*, translation so alive that it is always felt as a novel
creation, so one cannot recognise the individual excellence
of Henryson without awareness of Chaucer's poem.
'Quha wait gif all that Chaucer wrait wes trew?', he asks,
and proceeds with his own invented tale of the latter fate of
the character who, he rightly perceived, was more suitable
as the subject of a tragic treatment than the wholly worthy
but merely pathetic Troilus.

It is commonly said that in his choice and treatment of
theme the Scots poet intended a criticism of the Englishman's poem. An intention of this kind might equally be
read into the relationship of 'The Taill of Schir Chanticleir and the Foxe' and *The Nonne Preestes Tale*, or that of
Troilus and Criseyde and *Il Filostrato*, but it is creation, not
criticism, that Boccaccio's successors have in mind. They
simply have something different to do and say, naturally
of differing value. Chaucer writes a love story of alternating unhappiness, happiness, unhappiness, with a concluding Boethian counsel (a remarkable mosaic of transla-
tions)[1] of acceptance of, and detachment from, the
unlucky experience. Henryson does not write a love story.
That part of his heroine's career is a *datum* from which he
proceeds to another tale; she has rejected one lover, been
rejected by another (perhaps by yet others), 'fra luiffaris
left and all forlane' [abandoned], now she will learn
terribly that love is indeed not for her, and die, so to speak,
without benefit of Boethius.

An understanding of what happens and what is said in
Henryson's masterpiece is so essential to a full appreciation, and is so often incomplete or quite wanting in the
several commentaries,[2] that an interpretative retelling of
the tale must be attempted here. Only with such an understanding can one pretend to consider critically, in its most
exacting sense, the term 'tragedie' applied by the author
to his poem. Henryson himself observes that as *Troilus and*

Criseyde is the tragedy of Troilus, this is the tragedy of Cresseid. Yet the description in the title is 'Testament', though strictly this should apply only to lines 575–88. No contradiction is involved. As Christ left his testament in the instructive example of his life, so does Cresseid leave hers in the example of a very different but also dear-bought experience. The overtly Christian reference of the title reminds the reader, despite the pagan setting of the tragedy, what kind of judgments and sympathies is expected from him.

The beginning follows a method learned from the autobiographical *Kingis Quair*, and not from those poems of Chaucer which offer the perfunctory excuse of a dream. Such a method allows the poet to infect the reader with his own serious involvement in the subject. We are not, therefore introduced directly to Cresseid but to the poet explaining to his audience of the future the circumstances in which he came to tell her story. Of course, they carry a warning; they foreshadow hostile aspects of the world in which Cresseid has her tragic experience, and in the sympathetic character of the author hint at the attitudes he will develop in the story.

The weather when he began to write happened to be of the kind that might well turn one's thoughts to a 'cairful dyte'—he does not say that there was ever a conventional equivalence in weather for such writing, only it seems to him, considering the events he is to narrate, that it would be quite understandable if there were. It was extreme, 'fervent',[3] one might have said unnatural for that season, hail and northern winds hurling themselves into the spring scene, so that the watching poet shivered in his cold oratory. The planet of love, 'fair Venus the bewtie of the nicht', rose in unnatural 'oppositioun' to the sun then setting—Henryson, obviously knowledgeable in astrology, much as he disapproved of its destinal claims,[4] would have known that the planet could not be so placed, but the coincidental departure of the life-giving sun had its significance. The observer was there to pray Venus, 'My faidit hert of lufe scho wald mak grene', for in that respect too nature was against him. An ageing if not old poet, he still knew desire, but no longer with the potency and excitement of youth, 'Of quhome the blude is flowing in ane rage'. Coldness outside, coldness within, he reflected, but there was the consolation ('remeid') of warm fire, warming drink that recalled the ancient jest 'help be physike', and book to 'short' the winter-like night.

That night the book chosen was *Troilus and Criseyde* but, of course, the reader will know Chaucer's story of the disappointed Troilus and (it is implied) he will not know the other book, 'In quhilk I fand the fatall destenie/Of fair Cresseid that endit wretchitlie';[5] probably as unreliable a history as Chaucer's but it told what the great poet had omitted—and here one recognises the characteristic direction of Henryson's genius, the basic spring of all his 'inventioun', pity—'quhat distres scho thoillit [suffered] and quhat deid' [death].

The introduction is over and has served its artistic and philosophic purpose; the setting of the tale is itself an exposition of the contraries of life that Cresseid's fate will illustrate; a series of oppositions and contradictions, spring with winter, love and growth with coldness and sterility, youth with age, 'worthie glorious Chaucer' and a nameless poet with a darker tale to tell, truth and fiction. The writer has shown his understanding of Fortune's world, Fortune whom he elsewhere called 'haill maistres and leidar of the dance',[6] and the reader will, or should, share that understanding as Cresseid's tragedy now unfolds.

Henryson's narrative begins with a style of unsparing directness that has no parallel in poetry and calls for comment. He seems to contain himself, not to allow feeling to extend beyond the stated fact, dissipate itself in any irrelevance of adornment or distraction of rhythmical indulgence. The result is the utter attention of the reader

to what is being said, its gravity, his awareness of the
speed with which the rapid succession of statements
moves towards a conclusion that is increasingly weighted
with meaning and felt to be inevitable. It is a style that
creates continuous expectation and is always intense,
equal to its painful matter. The opening statement of
Cresseid's situation illustrates this well enough; seeming
by its bareness to avoid feeling, it is charged with feeling.

> Quhen Diomeid had all his appetyte,
> And mair, fulfillit of this fair ladie,
> Upon ane uther he set his haill delyte,
> And send [sent] to hir ane lybell [note] of
>   repudie,
> And hir excludit fra his companie.
> Than desolait scho walkit up and doun,
> And, sum men sayis, into the court commoun.

The force of contemptuous satiety in the tag 'And mair' is
felt by every reader. The absoluteness of the dismissal is
conveyed by legal terms, 'lybell of repudie' (from the
Vulgate Bible, *Matthew* V. 31 etc.), 'excludit', 'desolait'.
The force of this last word would be particularly
appreciated by Scots; in the beginning of Barbour's *Bruce* it
is said that with the death of Alexander III and a disputed
succession Scotland lay 'desolait', that is, without king or
Guardian. The picture of a Cresseid who 'walkit up and
doun', distracted and directionless, reinforces the
meaning of the previous term and brings in the idea of
despair. In the last line the qualification, 'sum men sayis',
given to the report of her final degradation, contrives both
to query the report and to strengthen its likliehood. The
felt reluctance to add this charge hints at the poet's
sympathies; and the implied query, like the earlier expression of doubts about the accounts of both Chaucer and the
author under review, suggesting a concern with the truth
of events, that justice be done to Cresseid, touches an issue
that becomes increasingly important in the story. *Multum*

in parvo seems to be the principle that governs Henryson's mode of expression.

In the next two stanzas the pity is more overt. The poet's sense of life's painful necessities, so often articulated in the *Fabillis*, is heard in the exclamation, 'how was thow fortunait!' [fortuned]; not Cresseid but her enforced way of life, her 'foull plesance', is exclaimed against. Weakness she showed, yes, but the intelligent, modest and delightful woman (praised as such by Chaucer, V. 816–20) she was before uncaring Fortune put her 'in sic distress' is not to be forgotten; her destitution should be considered, pity and not heartless words is what the case requires.

Why such understanding charity should be considered 'morally imbecilic', as it is by Denton Fox, escapes the present writer. Professor Fox, in his introduction to the poem, is so disturbed by his discovery of inconsistent attitudes in the commentary that he invents a sentimentally muddled narrator for the first part of the story, who makes an unsignalled exit after a characteristically foolish protest against the worsening fortune of Cresseid, to make way for an intelligently severe poet whose late arrival is equally unsignalled. Such an interpretation, if textually based—of course, it is not—would mean not only a muddled half-time narrator but also a muddled poet and poem; but we can discount it except as testimony to Henryson's admitted avoidance of simple, unqualified judgments.

Significant simplicity is, however, the very effective principle of Henryson's scene-setting for the tale, as it was for the introduction. A good Aristotelian he eschews the multiplicity of detail, circumstance and conversation, in Chaucer's narrative, a method that suits the novelistic and discursive bent of the Englishman's genius but does not allow concentration on the few arresting and meaningful pictures that alone concern the tragic artist. (Naturally, Chaucer is more taken up with his original contribution to

Boccaccio's story, the painful and sometimes comic complication of the hero's winning of love, than with his much less original account of its loss.) Ignoring this essential of dramatic presentation, J. A. W. Bennett can actually object to what he considers a slightness and vagueness in the topographical information provided by Henryson— 'In *Troilus* we always know precisely where we are: it has even been possible to make plans of Chaucer's Troy and of the chief houses in it'.[7] But where the respective houses of Troilus, Pandarus and Criseyde etc. stand concerns no serious-minded reader; what happens in these merely notional residences does.

As for Henryson's few but sufficient signs of location, so far from being distractingly vague and 'perplexing', they give quite clear and consistent instruction, just so much as the movement of action to its tragic close requires. The discarded Cresseid, 'Richt privilie, but [without] fellowschip, on fute', leaves Diomede's Greek camp, naturally enough called a 'toun' after ten years of siege-war—in Scots a 'toun' could be anything from a farm-house to a city—for the other 'toun' that to her seeming is 'far off' but is only two miles distant, where stands her father's temple or 'kirk' of Cupid and Venus. It is in the private oratory of his adjoining house that she will complain and have the savage answer of the gods; from the back gate of the house that Calchas will escort his stricken daughter to the hospital, a half-mile away in a 'village' (a small group of houses) 'at the tounes end', towards Troy; and in this last position, begging by the wayside, that Troilus returning from a raid on the Greek camp will pass her unknowingly, later in Troy to receive the message of her death. Few scenic arrangements for such a purpose could be simpler, apart from the single-scene setting of Greek tragedy. When the messenger seeks Troilus with the news of her death, something like a destinal circle (a concept familiar to Henryson from his reading of *The Kingis Quair*)[8] can be simply visualised.

A few of Bennett's Bentleian (his own word) objections and misreadings may be conveniently disposed of here, some merely by way of re-statement. He wonders that a mirror should be available to Cresseid in an oratory, though in Henryson's day small polished hand mirrors were everyday attachments to the girdle of any lady of quality, and had indeed been in use in Scotland since the eighth century at latest. He asks why the pagan priest should assume that his daughter in the oratory is on her knees, 'on grouf', at prayer; how can he know this if the door is shut? He thinks that pagan gods were not supposed to know the heart's 'intent', as the father expects them to do; sees no need for secrecy when the leprous Cresseid is led to the hospital; asks why she needs to beg when her father has promised to send 'sum meit'—however unexplained this point may be, the fact is that lepers did need to beg and only received meat or fish that was not fresh.[9] He has the same difficulty as Fox with the 'imbecilic' pleas that sympathy be shown to an unfortunate Cresseid, and can only assume that Henryson, blindly and unintelligently following the master, does not perceive that Chaucer pities without excusing her. He finds Cresseid to be talking non-sense when she says of Troilus's consideration for women that he 'helpit thair opinion'—which means, of course, 'took their side against slanderers'. He observes that bequeathing her goods to her fellow lepers 'is hardly the striking proof of her sincerity and unselfishness that Tillyard takes it to be: they would share them in any event'. This needs no comment. The amused reader of Bennett's commentary will at least agree that its writer is not in sympathy with Henryson.

Turning from this Bentleian interlude, one finds that the same sympathy the poet had vainly asked from Venus, and had given to Cresseid, is shown by Calchas to the Prodigal, as she may be called at least for the destitution that makes her seek her father's house:

"Douchter, weip thow not thairfoir.
Peraventure all cummis for the best.
Welcum to me! Thow art full deir ane gest."

Any reading that is not in this spirit will go against the
intention of Henryson. The father's statement that is also
a question, "Perhaps everything is for the best", brings in
the central issue of tragedy as Shakespeare and Milton
would have conceived it, divine justice. It is a question that
was real also to Chaucer, but his practical and conventional mind turned away from pursuing it with the
intensity that Henryson permitted to himself and his creations. Theseus in *The Knightes Tale*, saying 'whoso
gruccheth ought he dooth folye', presents the image that
Chaucer would always wish to maintain in his poetry. If
Troilus curses the gods, among them Cupid, V. 204–10, it
is 'in his throwes frenetike', and we are not asked to
consider him seriously in the rôle of rebel and blasphemer.

It is otherwise with Cresseid. Her blasphemy is the
centre of the poem, prepared for by making her father
priest to the two gods she blasphemes,[10] its time of
utterance a 'solempne day' when all but she are at
worship, its wording at that moment given a passion and
articulateness that European writers had not allowed to
the religious rebel; her momentary outcry weighted in a
hitherto unexampled way by the cosmic significance conferred by the subsequent scenes, and her attitude apparently maintained through suffering, and only abandoned
with the heartbreak of her unknowing encounter with
Troilus. A dying repentance that brings no peace of mind
has the effect, unintended as it may be, of leaving the
protest unsilenced and not fully answered at the close of
her story.

Her moment of rebellion makes its strong impression,
not only for the reasons given above but because of the
sense of the poet's serious involvement in her complaint,
his dramatic presentation of it as a charge of injustice

brought against an unseen court and supported by
specified wrongs: the gods have lied to her and betrayed
her; it is they and not she who have to justify themselves. I
quote the circumstance and charge in full.

> As custome was, the pepill far and neir
> Befoir the none unto the tempill went
> With sacrifice, devoit in their maneir;
> Bot still Cresseid, hevie in hir intent,
> Into the kirk wald not hirself present,
> For giving of the pepill ony deming
>   [occasion for talk]
> Of hir expuls fra Diomeid the king;
>
> Bot past into ane secreit orature
> Quhair scho micht weip hir wofull desteny.
> Behind hir bak scho closit fast the dure
> And on hir kneis bair [on the floor] fell doun
>   in hy: [threw herself down]
> Upon Venus and Cupide angerly
> Scho cryit out and said on this same wyse,
> "Allace that ever I maid you sacrifice!
>
> Ye gave me anis ane devine responsaill
>   [answer to prayer]
> That I suld be the flour of luif in Troy;
> Now am I maid ane unworthie outwaill, [outcast]
> And all in cair translatit is my joy.
> Quha sall me gyde? Quha sall me now convoy,
> Sen I fra Diomeid and nobill Troylus
> Am clene excludit as abject [cast-off] odious?
>
> O fals Cupide is nane to wyte [blame] bot thow,
> And thy mother, of lufe the blind goddes!
> Ye causit me alwayis understand and trow
> The seid of lufe was sawin in my face,
> And ay grew grene throw your supplie and grace:
> Bot now, allace that seid with froist is slane,
> And I fra luifferis left and all forlane!"

The passion of any tragic response to conceived wrongs or painful mystery should be felt as a voice of strength and not weakness, and in the angry hurt of this complaint there is nothing of Chaucer's 'ferfulleste wicht', nor of his lamenting Troilus, whose personality, weak as the impression it made always was, runs out in words. Anger there is in Cresseid, yet I use the phrase 'angry hurt' advisedly, for commonly in Scots 'angerly' means 'in suffering', and it is, above all, suffering that speaks. Cresseid, we are told, 'Usit . . . hir prayeris for to say' in that room, but now she has not come to pray.

In realistic terms the charge is that the gods (Nature) gave her the beauty that should have made her the most loved of women, but things have turned out differently; it was a lying gift. She still has the beauty but love has proved blind to it. It was a commonplace of poetry that love was blind, not like justice from impartiality, but from arbitrariness—Gower's priest observes that it favours the undeserving as often as the deserving—a working of chance; so it is against a world of blind chance, Fortune, that Cresseid complains. The theme is in the poem's opening description of a hostile, unnatural Nature, with the planet Venus not warm but cold, in opposition to natural desire.

Literary reminiscence enters the last stanza of the complaint, possibly of Gower's Thisbe complaining of Venus and Cupid in words that could be read as representing both as blind, certainly, as Bennett points out, of the *Roman de la Rose*, whether in the original or Chaucer's translation, 1563–1617: there the well of love makes always green the grass about it so that it may not die in winter; it is a 'mirrour perilous' showing the irresistible face of love, and Cupid 'Hath sowen there of love the seed'. A picture very different from Henryson's winter scene watched by a poet whose 'faidit hart of luif' is given no chance to grow green, and very different from the experience of Cresseid! Readers of so popular a work as the *Roman* would be expected to appreciate the irony of the contrast, and recognise the theme of lucky and unlucky loves that both allusions illustrate.

That Cresseid has, in fact, already contracted the ravaging disease from which she is to die, and that this is in some sort venerial, as Professor MacQueen asserts, is a peculiarly modern debasement of the heroine's situation, quite unevidenced by the text.[11] He makes much of the privacy that she seeks, but Henryson attributes this only to hurt pride, the desire to keep secret 'hir expuls fra Diomeid the King'; her father sees nothing of this ravaging disease in her face when she comes home. Also, at this stage to read such a condition into her winter of discontent is to give the lie to the simply moving explanation that she gives to Calchas, "He wox werie and wald of me no moir"; worse, it devalues the scene that is to follow, the horrified consternation of both daughter and father. Of course, MacQueen, also Fox, will intrude the same explanation into that scene, and see the story in terms of simple cause and effect, retribution for physical and moral defect, in an ordered world where the disastrous Fortune and 'mischance' that troubled Henryson and engaged his sympathy for Cresseid has little place.

The event that follows Cresseid's 'blasphemy' makes visible the unseen court against which she had spoken, and so impresses on us the cosmic dimension of her challenge, her charge of injustice. The court is convoked by 'Cupid the King ringand ane silver bell/Quhilk men micht heir fra hevin unto hell'. Cupid whose power goes everywhere and who can indeed call men to heaven or to hell. He is certainly not, as Fox would suggest, 'amor che muove il sole e tutte le stelle', the divine Mover of the universe. He is the classical Cupid, as Henryson's contemporary Thomas Waleys describes him, *amor carnalis filius voluptatis*,[12] 'love of the flesh, the son of pleasure', and as such he gets 'litill reverence' from cold and churlish Saturn, the eldest member of the court. In a real sense this is the story of Saturn and Cresseid. The arrows at the god's belt, 'Fedderit with ice and heidit with hailstanis' prefigure his judgment and recall the 'Schouris of haill' when the poet began his writing. Farthest from life as men know it on earth, he none the less arrives first, and it is in the order indicated by his arrival that the other planetary gods come to claim their seat.

Each one is portrayed according to the character given him in astrology, the science that pretended to explain men's earthly fortunes by reference to the positioning of these charactered planets—Ptolemy called his book *The Judgments*. Yet vividly distinct as each description is, and more appreciated for the significant touches with each fresh reading, they are not of equal significance for the story. Jupiter, Saturn's brilliant son who wears the colours of green and gold that are symbolic of life and prosperity, is said to carry 'ane groundin [polished] speir,/Of his father the wraith fra us to weir' [ward off], but he makes no defence here, and is only a presence, neither acting nor speaking in the assembly. Similarly Mars 'the god of ire' may enter rattling his sword and blowing the horn that calls to strife and war, but again is only an appearance; as also is bright Phoebus driving his four-horsed chariot, without whom 'Must all ga die that in this warld is wrocht'. With the picture of Venus, though she will leave the speaking to her son, meaning with a direct bearing on Cresseid's plight such as Saturn's portrait carried re-enters the scene. This Venus is not the goddess of convention, for example, Chaucer's goddess 'naked, fletyng in a see'; menace prevails in her aspect, she is a manifestation of the greatest of the gods and goddesses, less openly represented by the others, Fortune. She appears as does Fortune in all the accounts, as a series of contraries.[13] Her dress is parti-coloured like a fool, one side a wanton green, the other a deathly black. Her hair has the golden colour of prosperity and truth, but is belied by the face that shows a perpetual change of mood.

Smiling, angry, weeping, variant in everything but incon-
stancy, as is all human love, like life itself, 'Now grene as
leif, now widderit and ago', she embodies the contrary
experiences of love and life that the poet of the introduction had known in his own person, and against which
Cresseid now protests. The many-talented Mercury who
follows is equally the creature of Fortune's various world—
recalling Dryden's satiric portrait of Buckingham who,
'in the course of one revolving moon/Was chemist,
statesman, fiddler and buffoon'. He is a silver-tongued
orator, a facile poet, a natural master of the ceremonies, a
liar and, conceivably, a pander. Seventh and last of the
arrivals is young 'Lady Cynthia', almost as foolish and
sinister in her appearance as Venus, horned, leaden-
complexioned as Saturn, 'swiftest in hir spheir'; what
light she has is borrowed from her brother the sun.

If the members of the Convocation are unequal in
importance for the occasion, yet the attendance of all is
necessary, for in their astrological characters they symbolise the totality of man's physical experience, his
experience of Fortune's world. With the exception of
Jupiter and Phoebus they are not impressive or genial
figures, and the overall effect is caricature. It is something
of a mock parliament that convenes. This is as it should
be, for in many respects it is a foolish world that they
represent. No sensible man would suppose, yet it has been
usually supposed, that in their collective 'wisdom' they
could set up as spokesmen for God. If King Cupid
presides, that is because on earth at least he is as physical
a power as the others, and the case specially concerns that
part of experience he governs so blindly.

The speech as prosecutor that Henryson writes for him
has its appropriate mixture of half-truths and unconscious
ironies. His opening proposition is sound enough, in
blaming him Cresseid blames all the gods of her world.
That Cresseid has called his mother 'Ane blind goddes . . .
that micht nocht se' is, on the other hand, no more than

the truth if she is at all like the Venus Henryson has described—it would have been unwise for him to put her into the witness-box at this point. That he, Cupid, who gave her the beauty that made her 'the flour of lufe', the best loved of women, should be held responsible for her immoral loves he rightly rejects—after all, morals are not his concern. His claim that the jury of seven are 'Participant of devyne sapience' is obviously untrue in the sense that he intends, though they are, oddly enough, the creations of divine wisdom. His concluding advice, "Thairfoir, ga help to revenge I yow pray", is certainly not Christian, but quite in keeping with the powers that Fortune possesses. His preceding sentence splutters with offended vanity, "Was never to goddes done sic violence!"

In this speech one cannot help feeling that Henryson's *penchant* for the absurd comes near to spoiling the overall serious effect intended. That danger, however, is quickly removed when the plausible Mercury—'Honest and gud and not a word culd lie'—gives the counsel that brings the two patron planets of disease in judicial conjunction. Their separate readings of the sentence are given with overwhelming solemnity and finality. It will be enough to quote the last lines of Cynthia's judgment:

> "Quhair thow cummis ilk man sall fle the place;
> Thus sall thow go begging fra hous to hous
> With cop and clapper lyke ane lazarous."

Who has given the judgment I have stated? Not 'devyne sapience', unless we see this in all the events of this world of Fortune. Yet there is indeed an order of law in her physical world that is truly the work of God. As Henryson observes in *The Preaching of the Swallow*, 'God in all His werkis wittie is'; but to a large extent God has left Fortune or Chance a free hand in her operations, so far as the individual's health and happiness are concerned and, as Henryson also remarks in the same poem, not being God man feels its touch and suffers painfully. Human defect does not, of course, exempt him from moral responsibility; he can still value ordinary prudence, and has his share of the higher wisdom to modify, if never remove, his vulnerability to sin, so that he may find transient joy in this world, eternal, perhaps, in the next. Cresseid's passions have made her wholly vulnerable to her 'mischance' and she suffers accordingly. What her response to ill luck will be is what will determine any happiness she knows in this life as in the next. It is with that response that the rest of her story as Henryson tells it is concerned. Meanwhile, in the gods of Fortune she has once more, as when she was sent to the Greek camp, and was deserted by Diomede, encountered bad luck, and deserves our pity. As the poet says, that is one quality that cannot be looked for in Fortune, who has no more to do with it than has Cupid with morals.

Henryson's protest against Saturn's doom is thus a human voice that the gods (not God) cannot and should not be expected to understand. To ask justice of them as Cresseid has done, or pity as Henryson now does, is to be as unreasonable as the gods themselves, but in tragedy questions must be put and human values illustrated.

> O cruell Saturn, fraward and angrie,
> Hard is thy dome and to malitious!
> On fair Cresseid quhy hes thow na mercie,
> Quhilk was sa sweit, gentill and amorous
>   [loving]?

The pity already shown by the priest Calchas, and now Henryson's, is, of course, the Christian reaction. It is right in itself irrespective of the sufferer's faults. None the less, the implicit extension of the protest to God himself must be recognised. The man who made such a passionate demand for justice in the *Fabillis*, and who tended the lazar-house in Dunfermline, could not help finding a real question to be asked, and sometimes finding it hard to believe, with Calchas, that 'all cummis for the best'. One remembers the advice in the *Preiching*, 'Trow fermelie and lat all resoun be'.

The particular doom, or chance as I have argued it to be, of leprosy was sometimes in the textbooks, rarely in recorded cases, associated with venereal disease; then only because of one or two shared symptoms, for example, a hoarse voice; but it was never directly attributed to that, a distinction Professor Fox does not note in his citation of the textbooks. If Cresseid's leprosy had derived from her way of life, there is no reason why Henryson should not have said so. Saturn's special connection with the disease—the moon's conjunction is needed only because she is the planet of swift or sudden change—was a commonplace of semi-astrological treatises on astronomy such as that of the universally read Sacrobosco.[14] No Scotsman would have represented this well known affliction of the national hero, Bruce, as a consequence of his casual love-affairs! Barbour (II. 174) attributes it to a Saturnian enough aspect of his strenuous life, the cold he suffered lying out in the hills.

The case of Bruce is interesting for the other reason given for it, his sacrilegious breaking of faith with his rival Comyn, when in a moment of rage he stabbed the latter at their appointed meeting in the Friary at Dumfries. The curing of the emperor Constantine's leprosy when he adopted the true faith was seen in the same light. And one may cite the very popular romance of *Amis and Amiloun* in which a falsely taken oath of a religous character brings leprosy to the perjurer. In the Bible Gehazi is one of several examples of the same punishment for a sacrilegious abuse. In the early sixteenth-century Scots romance, *The History of a Lord and his Three Sons*, though there is no religious context, a broken promise makes the heroine suffer in the same way. Leprosy, therefore, is the symbolically appropriate form of the latest and worst 'mischance' to befall Troilus's perjured love. Yet it is not so much its reference to promise-breaking, as its meaning

for a woman to whom beauty and the protective lover it
brought meant so much, that suggests it; she will indeed
now, as she had already complained, be "fra luifferis left
and all forlane" [neglected].

The one respect in which Fortune could be imagined to
have a right of complaint, and then, of course, not in her
own person but as a creation of God, is the demand that
she be accepted as the amorally changeful being that she
is. Failure to accept her does become rebellion against
God, and Cresseid may be deemed to have committed that
sin. By presenting her misery as the decree of incompetent
and very suspect judges, as he did in the trial scenes of his
tales, 'The Scheip and the Doig' and 'The Wolf and the
Lamb', Henryson has secured our sympathy but put at
risk our recognition of her sin. The rebellion is, of course, a
greater matter in its religious implications than the
infidelity to Troilus, in which it was possible to see simply
an unlucky if erring girl: 'how was thou fortunait!' (how
things turned out for you!). How the rebellious spirit
responds to this most unhappy of predicaments, one that
is indeed pure mischance, is the subject to be treated in the
ensuing scenes of the 'tragedie', though it will be the
memory of one lost love that finally kills her.

The treatment proceeds in a series of brief, almost
cryptic, expressions of her plight, a method whose efficacy
only the great tragic poets appreciate, and contain themselves enough to practice. Cresseid looks in her hand-
mirror:

> And quhen scho saw hir face sa deformait,
> Gif scho in hart was wa eneuch God wait!
>
> Weiping ful sair, "Lo, quhat it is", quod scho,
> "With fraward [hostile] language for to mufe and
>   steir [rouse]
> Our craibit [soon angered] goddis".

Her father, expecting her at supper, sends a boy from the

hall to complain that she makes her prayers too long,
"The goddis wait all your intent full weill," as indeed they
do, and is himself sent for:

> He luikit on hir uglye lipper face
> The quhylk befor was quhite as lillie-flour;
> Wringand his handis oftymes he said allace
> That he had levit to se that wofull hour!
> For he knew weill that thair was na succour
> To hir seiknes, and that dowblit his pane.
> Thus was thair cair aneuch betwix thame twane.

The sense of two persons isolated in a shared grief for
which there are no, or only helpless, words has never been
better conveyed. That it is a family scene makes the understanding between the two more imaginable, and more
poignant in its effect, and the first reported words of
Cresseid have the more impact, "Father I wald not be
kend". The details that he takes her by a 'secreit yett'
[privy gate] to her destination, and disguised, indicate the
exclusion from society that this time is permanent.

Henryson's awareness, uncommon for his age, of the
importance of scene-setting, particularly of the way in
which circumstances of time and colour can distance, and
give, as it were, a window through which to look at events
that should not be seen too closely, suggesting, however
briefly, the universal frame in which they occur, is
illustrated in the first two lines of the stanza that precedes
'The Complaint of Cresseid':

> The day passit and Phebus went to rest,
> The cloudis blak ouirquhelmit all the sky.

It is mood-setting, and it carries the sense of time endured.

To some extent because of the effective brevity of what
went before, but also because it partly takes us away from
the Cresseid of the present, and the world she remembers
is now so far off and unreal, the 'Complaint' seems too
long, too wordy in its questioning, 'Where has yesterday

gone?' It is a real question and nobody knows the answer, so it seems pointless, if natural. Villon cannot go on asking the question, neither can Henryson. Yet one does pause at lines that are immediate and vivid enough to be felt to speak from Cresseid's present—

> "Under the eirth God gif I gravin wer
> Quhair nane of Grece nor yit of Troy
>   micht heird!'"

> "Quhair thou was wont full merrily in May
> To walk and tak the dew be it was day,
> And heir the merle and mavis, mony ane."

> "And for thy bed tak now ane bunche of stro".

In a poem of only 616 lines it is quite surprising how many persons other than the heroine make an effective entrance, however briefly some of them stay with us. The poet, of course, stays with us longest, and however fictitiously he may introduce himself to us I do not believe that he shares his guiding rôle with the narrator that Professor Fox and some others have imagined him to follow. It is true that Diomede is not allowed to speak for himself but the man whose 'appetyt, and mair' was satiated on Cresseid is an even clearer presence than he is in Chaucer. There is Cresseid's father, there are the gods (particularly memorable among them Saturn and Mercury), the lepers, and later there will be Troilus. Unlike Diomede and the gods, who are a party to themselves, the others show the virtue of pity, and now it is shown, along with a terrible commonsense, in the 'lipper-lady' who does and says so much in a few lines. In the night, as Cresseid laments, the lady rises from her straw-bed and goes to her:

> "Quhy spurnis thow againis the wall
> To sla thyself and mend nathing at all?

Sen thy weiping doubillis bot thy wo,
I counsall the, mak vertew of ane neid—
To leir to clap thy clapper to and fro,
And live eftir the law [ways] of lipper leid". [folk]

The 'vertew' accords with the good Boethian advice offered by Chaucer's Theseus to Palamon and Emily—who after several years are still decently mourning Palamon's dead friend and rival Arcite, and now are to be married—"Thanne is it wysdom, as it thynketh me,/To maken vertu of necessitee", an odd introduction to a marriage; but the very different circumstances and practical meaning in Cresseid's case seem to mock the advice. Henryson would have had to say the same thing, perhaps with the same thought, to more than one newcomer to his hospital, another addition to the living dead, as they were regarded in law. His recurring theme of driving need is here again. Cresseid listens because she has to, and for 'cauld and hounger sair' joins the lepers' begging forays in the countryside.

What are her thoughts about her condition, other than her regrets for the past and submission to the present? One might say that despair had quenched the bitterness of her rebellion, but there is no evidence that she repents it. On the contrary, the phrase 'Thair was na buit' [help for it] states only that protest is seen as pointless. In Henryson's poetic world it would seem that physical need and physical distress teach only lessons of the same order; they do not make one better and wiser; at best they teach resignation to the unamendable. In this respect he differs from those moralists (among them even poets) who wish to think that physical deprivation should confer spiritual gifts. It is from a different and higher order of suffering that Cresseid (like Lear) learns something about herself and what brought her to where she is, the recognition of her own part in that process.

The 'recognition' scene that follows is the most moving

and memorable of its kind in literature. It works in that way partly because it is not a recognition scene but a scene that suggests the recognition of what in happier circumstances there might have been. Lessing observes, "that is most fruitful of effect which leaves freest play to the imagination', and this treatment certainly allows such free play. The lepers, except for Cresseid who sits apart, a disinterested onlooker, run to cry "part of your almousdeid", as they see a company of soldiers, Troilus leading them, return from a day of triumph in the field. He has not heard of her leprosy.

> Than to thair cry nobill Troylus tuk heid;
> Having pietie, neir by the place can pas
> Quhair Cresseid sat, not witting quhat scho was.

> Than upon him scho kest up baith hir ene—
> And with ane blenk it come into his thocht
> That he sumtime hir face befoir had sene,
> Bot scho was in sic plye he knew hir nocht;
> Yit than hir luik into his mynd it brocht
> The sweit visage and amorous blenking
> Of fair Cresseid, sumtyme his awin darling.

> Na wonder was, suppois in mynd that he
> Tuik hir figure sa sone, and lo now quhy:
> The idole of ane thing in cace may be
> Sa deip imprentit in the fantasy
> That it deludis the wittis [senses] outwardly,
> And sa appeiris in forme and lyke estait
> Within the mynd as it was figurait.

> Ane sperk of lufe than till his hart can spring
> And kendlit all his bodie in ane fyre;
> With hait fevir ane sweit and trimb[i]ling
> Him tuik, quhill he was reddie to expyre;
> To beir his scheild his breist began to tyre;
> Within ane quhyle he changit mony hew.
> An nevertheless not ane ane-uther knew.

It has been asked why Cresseid, who looks up at Troilus does not know him, and has to be told by 'a lipper man'. The ordinary helmet of the poet's day did not conceal the face, and we shall later find her writing, so that we are left with the simplest and most effective interpretation, suggested by what we already know of her state of mind, and by her apartness from the noisy crowd: looking indifferently at the passing knight she did not see him, saw only her inner grief. Unlike the knight there was no object of love in her thought to stir even a speculation about his identity. It is the case of Troilus that Henryson feels he must explain: the Cresseid he had lost was always before his eyes, an image of his grief—that is how Fulgentius illustrates the word 'idol' and Walter Bower, Henryson's countryman, in 1449 interprets it[15]—so that it needed only the slightest resemblance in the wayside figure to recall it, even while he knew it to be an illusion. The irony is that it is really Cresseid that he sees. Two inward-looking griefs meet without recognition. His finds itself suddenly intensified beyond control, and does not know why. The symbolic reason sometimes given for the failure of recognition, that they have grown spiritually such strangers to each other, suggests itself less readily than the more obvious one, though I do not think a symbolic reason is needed, that their fortunes in this world are now hopelessly separate. But this variety of possible reasons is just that desirable free play of speculation that Lessing had demanded of great conceptions.

It has been said, for example, by Bennett, that Henryson's Troilus is the courtly hero of Chaucer unchanged, as ever "gentill and fre", showing the same bounty in the gifts that he throws to the wayside Cresseid, but not only is the situation in which he shows his nobility beyond Chaucer's imagining, he makes a more mature impression; the 'sperk of lufe that till his hart culd spring' is given more restrained and therefore more effective expression, 'Within a quhyle he changit many hew'; and he has been given what was not in Chaucer's copious and facile nature to give, the language of silence, 'Than raid away and not ane word he spak'.

The cry of Cresseid when she knows the identity of the giver (which she had not thought to ask till then), "O fals Cresseid and trew knycht Troilus!", is her first criticism aimed at anything but Fortune, and it is a cry forced by the kindness that Fortune had not shown. That enigmatic force is still with us as a theme. And more than an admission of guilt, though it is that, it is a cry for fatal folly. True, she can now repent that the love she gave Troilus was so shallow, 'frivolous', a mere 'wantoness'—the word does not quite have its modern meaning—a happy excitement of the senses just as available in the arms of Diomede; but her regret is more for a virtue then unappreciated, that Fortune had since taught her to value most, the 'so greit humanitie' of the irrecoverable Troilus, and it is her loss of the 'protectour and defence' that most strikes home. Folly still more than guilt is her theme.

And it is this prudential lesson rather than some redemptive moral that she addresses to other women, "Lovers, be war and tak gud heid about/Quhome that ye lufe, for quhome ye suffer paine". Henryson's sympathetic pessimism allows her what seems a defence, an extension of the excuses that he has already made for her: she deserves 'wickit langage' (91) no more than most women; she will accuse only herself now, but "Thocht sum be trew, I wait richt few ar thay"; a man is indeed lucky if he finds such a love. It is and is not a defence. Mainly it is a factual comment on human nature that her experience gives her the authority to make, "Becaus I knaw the greit unstabilnes/Brukill als glas". She has come a long way to make this recognition in herself of what she once saw only in Fortune.

It is not a knowledge that can now help, and if it is penitence it brings no peace. The theme of her ending as Henryson treats it is loneliness. She knows the pangs of

despair (542–43), "with stormie stoundis [pains] stad . . .
full will of wane" [utterly lost], and this appears too in the
very brief testament that she writes, which gives its name
to the poem: to the leper folk her cup and clapper,[16] and,
to provide for her burial, the gold that Troilus threw in her
lap; to Troilus the ring that he once exchanged for hers, so
that he should know of her death; her soul to Diana who
haunts wildernesses:

> "My spreit I leif to Diane quhair scho
>   dwellis
> To walk with hir in waist woddis and
>   wellis". [streams]

In this last bequest the chaste huntress may or may not
symbolise the purity of Cresseid in another world, her
redemption, but if it does that world is cheerless and
empty and suggests more a hell of regrets. She dies on the
cry,

> "O Diomeid, thou hes baith broche and belt
> Quhilk Troylus gave me in tak[e]ning
> Of his trew lufe!"

Cresseid's death, like any death, does not end the dead
person's story, there is still what it means to others. What
it would mean to her father when the news reached him
can be imagined and need not be mentioned here, or to
Diomede, to whom it would mean nothing. But there was
her one-time lover in Troy, who still loved her and knew
nothing of all this, and who alone concerned the dying
Cresseid. She was buried 'withoutin ony tarying', as any
leper would be, and the news, with her ring, carried at
once to Troilus. For a moment we are moved to see
through his eyes the different Cresseid he knew, and hear
him say "I can no moir" ("There are no words for this"),
and make the one comment, much more than a judgment,
"Scho was untrew—and wo is me thairfor!"

Again the poet appears as the reporter of uncertain

tradition (it was all so long ago), a distancing device that
still suggests the interest of many men: 'Sum said' Troilus
had a tomb made for her, 'of merbell gray', and on it
inscribed in golden letters this 'schort conclusioun' of her
story, all that needed saying—

> Lo, fair ladies, Cresseid of Troyis toun,
> Sumtyme countit the flour of womanheid,
> Under this stane, lait lipper, lyis deid.

And for the fair ladies of the poet's day, who should look to
their honour and continued happiness, four lines; for
himself only 'Sen scho is deid I speik of hir no moir'. These
two last words recur in Henryson's verse as if the finality of
loss was always with him; so in the *Preiching* the Swallow
that would have saved takes her flight, 'bot I hir saw no
moir'. It is this conveyance of a sympathetic finality, and
not any fancied restoration of a disturbed order, that
supplies the element of catharsis in our response to
Henryson's tragedy.

In the appreciative interpretation of his art, the method,
meaning and effect, that has been offered here the progres-
sion of the poem has been adhered to. It remains to make a
comparative comment on the poetic novel which he did
not consider himself to be rivalling or criticizing, so different was its aim and character. *Troilus and Criseyde* does,
however, call itself a 'tragidie', as does the *Testament*.

Not only is the former not a tragedy in any sense that
the term will bear today; without radical innovation in its
story such as Henryson provides not Shakespeare himself
could have made it one. That the innocent hero survives
his loss, however sore the hurt, is not even the difficulty in
question. The difficulty is that the mere fact of his private
grief—at this stage Pandarus who had once been allowed
to act and talk him out of his leading rôle is only the
shadow of that grief—is all that makes him interesting;
and this leads to neither a serious protest against unjust
gods (mere names in a curse that is given no significance,

V. 206–10, but which Henryson noted) nor to a noble acceptance of an irremediable situation. Having pathetically waited for a more enterprising Criseyde, who has realistically decided to make for a new life, and sighed his soul towards the Grecian tents, he seeks a suicidal and ineffectual revenge on the quite irrelevant Diomede.

Whatever tragic effect implies, it requires some kind of resolution of the protagonist's problem and attitude. Given the courage to leave the direction of Boccaccio, Chaucer might have invented such a resolution and critical judgment would have been different; but he preferred to be the 'grant translateur', even finding other pieces to translate and so extend the aimless path. By the end of the poem Troilus and Criseyde have each become 'a lighte goost'; the smile that Chaucer lifts from one of his sources and fits on the face of the heavenly Troilus, like the grin of the celebrated Cheshire cat, is all that there is to him. The story, after all, was going nowhere, and is remembered for the very human quality it had before it got there. Boethius might have approved, no tragic artist could. Fortunately, the vagueness in which he left Criseyde's fate gave Henryson's tragic 'invention' its opportunity.

NOTES

1. See the notes of F. N. Robinson, *The Works of Geoffrey Chaucer*, 1957. To those who think I make too much of Chaucer the translator I recommend that they compare line by line the relevant passages in Boccaccio's *Filostrato* and *Teseide*, Dante, Lucan.
2. The important ones are: above all J. MacQueen, *op. cit*; then E. M. W. Tillyard, *Five Poems 1470–1870*, 1948, 5–29 (has a too 'orderly' view of the late fifteenth century and knows little of Scottish 'disorder'); A. C. Spearing, *Criticism and Medieval Poetry*, 1964; J. A. W. Bennett, 'Henryson's *Testament*: a flawed masterpiece', *Scottish Literary Journal*, I. no. 1, July 1974, 1–16 (possibly not a fully considered comment); essays by T. W. Craik and M. P. McDiarmid in *Bards and Makars Scottish Language and Literature*, ed. Aitken, McDiarmid, Thomson, Glasgow University Press, 1977.

3. Denton Fox, *Robert Henryson Testament of Cresseid*, 1968, has much information, little judgment. He reads 'fervent' as 'hot', but see Gregory Smith's edition (S.T.S.) for citation from William Stewart's *Croniklis of Scotland*, II. 337, 'The feruent frost so bitter wes'.

4. See *Orpheus and Erudices*, 559–70, on Ticius in hell because he sought to know 'quhat destany and werd/Prevydit war to every man in erd''. Barbour roundly denounces astrology.

5. *The Spectakle Of Luf* completed 10 July 1492, thoroughly derivative, uses Henryson, not some other book, for its reference to Cresseid's leprosy and her going 'commoun amang the Grekis'.

6. 'The Taill of the Lyoun and the Mous' 1604–5.

7. I am not sure how serious Bennett is in certain of his comments; his title (see note 2) does concede a 'masterpiece'.

8. See *The Kingis Quair of James Stewart*, ed. M. P. McDiarmid, 1973, p. 55.

9. On hospitals see D. E. Easson, *Religious Houses*; John Durkan, 'Care of the Poor: Pre-Reformation Hospitals', *Innes Review*, X. 268–80.

10. In Chaucer as a diviner of the future he is priest of Apollo. Chaucer makes little of the familial relationship.

11. MacQueen, *op. cit.*, p. 62.

12. *Metamorphosis Ovidiana*, publ. Francois Regnault (1515), fol. viii r. French versions were published at Bruges 1484, Paris 1494.

13. One account recently read by Henryson is in *The Kingis Quair*, sts. 159–61.

14. See Lynn Thorndike, *The Sphere of Sacrobosco and its commentators*, 1949, pp. 213, 214, 217.

15. Walter Bower, *Scotichronicon*, Lib. I, cap. 35: 'an idol which in Latin we call an image [though his word is *speciem*] of grief'. Henryson certainly read this since he quotes a Latin saying from *Soctichronicon* in the *Fabillis*.

16. begging bowl and the rattle to warn others.

CHAPTER VI

THE SHORTER POEMS AND
'ANE SCHORT CONCLUSIOUN'

Robert Henryson has often been spoken of as an 'impersonal' poet—for example by his modern countryman Edwin Muir who chose to find something of his own remote poetic personality in him—a voice in which the stability, faith and calm of the great medieval order, as ideally imaged in the doctrinal system for which Dante, it is said, spoke so serenely and Chaucer so happily, can still be heard. To the present writer no one of these poets speaks in quite that way. Certainly Henryson does not.

How much he reveals of himself and his deeply perturbed responses to experience we have seen in the longer poems already considered, and in the dozen or so short ones that he has left similar self-revelation adds to the understanding that should prepare us for a judgment on his work.

Stylistically their method is incantation, often supported by the sharp stress of alliteration, and it is only when they are so recited, aloud, as all poetry should be read, but especially that of his day, that they make their proper impression. It is a various sensibility that comes across, in one or two cases plainly indifferent to a commonplace and dutifully expressed matter, as in *The Want of Wyse Men*, *The Ressoning betwix Deth and Man*, *Agains Haisty Credence of Titlaris* [idle slanderers], and to a lesser extent *The Abbey Walk* ('Is nocht but casualitie and chance'), but in the others, considered together, exhibiting an alternating power, gentleness and deliberate homeliness, that commands respect and liking for both man and artist.

Here there is room only for a few appreciative notes.

Doubtless the most famous of them is the wistfully humourous *Robene and Makyne*. It has in mind the French Robin and Marie scene and was written to a song-tune of the 'It was a shepherd and his lass' type. The old-world alliterative diction of the opening (soon abandoned) helps to set the mood of 'pastourelle'. The sexually urgent Makyne expounds the 'ABC', as she calls it, of courtly love in a few imploring words: be bold, don't accept 'danger' [standoffishness], and having got your will be 'patient and previe'. Robene, who understands at least what action is expected of him, but is not in the appropriate mood, protests that his sheep will miss his care, and in any case what is this love she makes so much of—it is understood throughout that he has always understood what plain 'sex' is. He goes off and begins to feel that he does understand what love might mean. The situation of Burns's Duncan Gray and his Meg is reversed. It is the woman now who grows 'hale' as he grows 'sick'. But the scene is best played in Henryson's words—

> "Robene, thow hes hard soung and say
> In gestis and storeis auld,
> The man that will nocht quhen he may
> Sall haif nocht quhen he wald.
> I pray to Jesu, every day
> Mot eik thair cairis cauld,   [coldly answered]
> That first preisis with the to play   [make love]
> Be firth, forrest or fauld".   [sheep-cote]

> "Makyne, the nicht is soft and dry,
> The wedder is warme and fair,
> And the grene woid rycht neir us by
> To walk attour allquhair;
> Thair may na janglour [gossip] us espy
> That is to lufe contrair;
> Thairin Makyne, bath ye and I
> Unsene we ma repair".

"Robene, that warld is all away
And quyt brocht till ane end,
And nevir agane thairto perfay
Sall it be as thow wend."

Robene has not lost Erudices, and his story does not
end with quite the same meaning as that of Orpheus when
he leaves his love in hell and 'A wofull wedowe hamwart is
he went', but the stories have in common the 'no moir'
theme that has been noticed in other contexts too. Missed
chances of many kinds is certainly a preoccupation of the
poet, and the recurrence of the theme of sex does explain
something of his sympathy for both Orpheus and
Cresseid.

It recurs in his poems of age and death and in places
suggests language for his religious poems. It is directly
and frankly applied to his own case, as I believe, in what
may be the latest of his poems, and from the stated age of
the elder speaker, sixty seven, probably written about
1503, *The Ressoning betwix Aige and Yowth*. This has a sung
refrain, "O yowth be glaid into thy flowris [growth]
grene", set against another sung refrain "O yowth, thy
flowris fadis fellone [fearfully] sone!"; the joy of sex will go
and "thy manheid sall wendin [pass] as the mone". The
duet ends with the older singer watching the younger go
off angrily, but of the former it is said that he 'luche
[laughed] not but tuk his leif'. We are left with a listening
poet who merely repeats both refrains and says how well
the singers sang, 'triumphit in thair tone', leaving the
reader to his own considerations. Withdrawal without
judgment from a scene that, after all, needs only factual
statement, something in which Henryson excels, gives it
all the more meaning.

A similarly concerned poem that pretends to be a
farewell to youth without regrets is the song with this
delightful opening,

Intyl ane garth, under a reid roseir [rose-tree],

> Ane ald man and decrepit hard I sing,
> Gay was the noit, swet wes the voce and cleyr.
> It wes gret joy to heir of sic ane thing;

but the song that follows is completely without gaiety, and is worth mentioning here only for lines that show the comment on youth and passion towards the beginning of the *Testament* were indeed the poet's, and not from some fictional and reprehensible narrator:

> Can nane withstand the ragyne of his blud,
> Na yit be stabil on-til he agit be;
> Than in the thing that mast rajoisit he
> Nathing ramanys for to be callit his.

The Thre Deid-Pollis may also address itself to 'lusty gallands' and 'ladeis quhyte, in claithis corruscant' in precisely the fashion that John Knox used to the women in Queen Mary's ante-chamber, but is in the usual *memento mori* style, and is interesting only at points. The line, 'Your fingearis small, quhyte as the quhailis bane', is sensuously striking. The guessing game played by the three skulls with the fascinated observer is a macabre piece of wit:

> This questioun quha can obsolve lat se,
> Quhat phisnamour or perfyt palmester,
> Quha was farest or fowlest of us thre?
> Or quhilk of us of kin was gentillar?

It is possible that Henryson remembered (as did Hamlet) the same question being asked of Alexander by Diogenes.[1] But more macabre is Henryson's sense of a fitness in the question of the three skulls being answered by prayer to the Trinity, 'Thre knit in ane be perfyt unitie'.

The short poems that are purely religious in respect of a certain state of mind being induced, 'quyet in contemplacioun', not the unease of regret or disgust for human weakness, of course not protest, are few, and come as near to pure poetry as his intense and troubled response to experience ever allowed. They are *The Garmont of Gud Ladies*, *The Annunciation* and *The Bludy Serk*, and again I must repeat that for due appreciation they must be read as incantation, and with full awareness of the sophisticated simplicity that they cultivate.

The *Garmont* is a gracefully continued conceit relating each item of dress to an inner perfection of the woman that the lover desires to wed. What is extraordinary is that in spite of the itemized spirituality it remains a love poem. It has a muted passion and tenderness. There is a real woman being talked about, and these are the perfections that love would give her. It is only slowly that one realises that they are the listed virtues that a priest might recommend to a woman entering upon the holy state of matrimony, but it is still not a priest's poem but a lover's poem. From the first stanza of promise,

> Wald my gud lady [future wife] lufe me best
> And wirk efter my will,
> I suld ane garmond gudliest
> Gar mak hir body till.

there is an increment of feeling, longing, to the final stanza,

> Wald scho put on this garmond gay,
> I durst sweir by my seill
> That scho woir nevir grene nor gray
> That set hir half so weill.

Again, if more expectedly, one notes how Henryson succeeds in fusing the rhetoric of courtly love with that of Mariolatry in *The Annunciation*: love can perform such miracles.

> Forcy as deith is likand [pleasing] lufe
> Throuch quhome al bittir swet is;
> Nothing is hard, as Writ can pruf,
> Till him in lufe that letis [dwells].

Or again, 'The miraclis are mekle and meit [natural]/Fra luffis ryver rynnis'. There are hymns to the Virgin in Holland, Dunbar, Kennedy, and other Scots poets; this is much the best because it does not seem to try to outdo others in emotive rhetoric, and keeps to its simple but profound theme of love, whether divine or human, being naturally miraculous and creative.

In *The Bludy Serk* the poet turns Christ's dying for man's soul into a tale of old romance, almost a fairy-tale, and with corresponding manner: a prince saves a fair lady from a 'foule gyane', and makes a seemingly unreasonable request on his deathbed that if another wooer come she should think on his bloody mail-shirt and reject him. The manner of simple and sad romance is maintained in the *Moralitas* so that it too seems to belong to the original tale. One notes how it is a specially archaic word at the commencement of the last three lines that sharpens attention, conveys a change in the teller's mood, a new urgency; the minstrel has done with his tale and explanation, now he seizes his audience:

> Hend [courteous] men, will ye nocht herk?
> For his lufe that bocht us deir
> Think on the bludy serk!

If it may seem to some readers that the extreme Henryson who conceived the impassioned protests of the suffering Orpheus and rejected Cresseid, and whose bitter theme so often in the *Fabillis* was injustice endured by the weak and the poor, is little heard in these generally acquiescent, though sometimes troubled, poems, they should remember that it is his own plight, not that of others, that he is trying to accept, and the divine love and pity that on a few occasions is his theme agrees well enough with what he expected of attitudes to situations in the major poems. At all events, the voice of protest is very clear in *Ane Prayer for the Pest*.[2]

It begins in the same way as did the *Preiching*, stressing

God's perfect knowledge of all times, so, of course, he knows of our sins that deserve the punishment of this 'perrelus pestilens', and, of course, if he chooses, his mercy can save us. Christ died to save us from sin, but however great that may be 'Oure deid [death] ma nathing our synnis recompens'. And this appalling death can only endanger souls—

> Allais
> That we sowld thus be haistely put down,
> And dye as beistis without confessioun,
> That nane dar mak with uther residence!

God's law must be kept, violation punished, but it is easier to understand punishment of those in high places, responsible for seeing that it is kept, than such indiscriminate punishment. God is an unsuspect judge who will surely free us of this dread. If he must punish, why not by some other way, above all, 'Puneis with pety and nocht with violens!' The theme is justice, and the sights that daily met the poet's eyes on the streets of Dunfermline, during the greatest plague of the century, did not accord with any notion of divine justice that satisfied him. He prayed but he protested, as had Orpheus and Cresseid, not to mention the Lamb of the fables.

With this poem we look directly at the spiritual sources of his poetry, pity, desire for justice, at the basic theme, a world that does not make sense, that is comic or tragic, depending on which bit of its non-sense you choose to see. Sense is in another world. If you see the world in this way, and have the realistic temperament of Chaucer, you write about what is comic, or when you feel a serious comment must be made you write about what is pathetic, an experience such as that of Troilus. The Chaucerian philosophy would seem to give so much life, until you realise that it is only a half-life, and so would exclude the intensest and richest experiences of life, and so most of its greatest art. Doubtless that is why the Wife of Bath is by much the Englishman's greatest creation. She lives not only on the middle 'ground of experience but at its extremes, as do the greatest creations in literature. It is to the extremes that Henryson's genius naturally turns, where life takes on most meaning; and that is why his Cresseid and his intensely human beast-world, and his own poetic personality, ultimately have more significance for us, than does the work that he thought of when he spoke affectionately of 'worthie Chaucer glorious'.

Henryson like Dante not only has been in hell but has enjoyed a great deal of this upper world's beauty. A recurrent and always heartfelt word is 'joy'—'It was grit joy to him that luifit corne' (as it would shine in the fields of harvest-time), 'The hartlie joy, God geve ye had sene,', etc. Such enjoyment gives a keener voice to his griefs: 'It wes richt hert-sair for to see/That bludie boucheour beit thay birdis doun!', or the description of Troilus's love that seems to imply a thousand sad fables, 'Cresseid of Troyis toun'. He has many styles but the one that has greatness is the simple and the factual: 'For he knew weill that there was na succour/To hir seiknes, and that dowblit his pane./Thus was thair cair eneuch betwix thame twane.'

Reality is his theme, even in his most fantastic comedy, so that the comic artist always writes from a tragi-comic vision. As regards the presentation of his humanised animals and his people in situations that touch a question of justice, he has been accused of 'piling on the agony', but the language with which he gets his poignant effects—like his comic effects—is of the sparest, and the true occasion of the charge is the fact that his created world is felt to be so much more real than that of his predecessors.

The future of Henryson's reputation not only as a poet but a great poet is assured now that he begins to be better known, and we no longer talk about the stern schoolmaster of Dunfermline. The once neglected, now much loved, poet will have no difficulty in holding his place; in his own words—

The miraclis are mekle [many] and meit [true]
Fra luffis ryver rynnis:
The low [flame] of luf haldand the hete
Unbrynt full blithlie burns.

NOTES

1. Mentioned by Henryson's contemporary John Mair [Major] with the
   same reference to nobility. See John Major's *Greater Britain*, transl.
   Archibald Constable, 1892, p. 400.
2. On this plague see Chapter I, p. 12.